ALLAN W. JOHNSTONE

United States
Direct Investment in France:

An Investigation of the French Charges

The M.I.T. Press

MASSACHUSETTS INSTITUTE OF TECHNOLOGY
CAMBRIDGE, MASSACHUSETTS

280800

Foreword

M.I.T.'s Brooks Prize is awarded for the best Master's thesis submitted during the year to the faculty of the Alfred P. Sloan School of Management. The Prize, named for E. P. Brooks, the first Dean of the School, emphasizes the importance we place on the clear analysis and lucid presentation of complex management problems, which the thesis exercise represents. In 1964, the Prize was awarded for the thesis submitted by Allan W. Johnstone, a recipient of a Sloan Fellowship in Executive Development and a Master's candidate in the Alfred P. Sloan School of Management. This monograph, adapted by Mr. Johnstone from his thesis, is the second published in this series concerned with questions in the international field, a growing area of importance for American management and for students generally interested in industrialization and economic growth.

HOWARD W. JOHNSON
Dean, Alfred P. Sloan School of Management
Massachusetts Institute of Technology

Preface

"A good wine needs no bush." Allan Johnstone's informed and thoughtful study of American investments in France stands on its own feet as a contribution to knowledge and as a brilliant example of the scholarly work undertaken by the young businessmen who come to the Alfred P. Sloan School of Management of M.I.T. for a year of study. He has singled out a neuralgic issue in the field of international economic relations, and examined it carefully from the points of view both of American business and of French social, political, and economic interests. His acuity in choosing this problem has been underlined by the continued attention given to it in the last year in Franco-American economic relations.

Mr. Johnstone's year of study ended with his receipt of the Master of Science in Management in June of 1964; the inexorable requirements of production mean that he closed the books on thesis material earlier in that year. Accordingly his treatment does not touch on one form the issue now takes: the question of whether American investments in Europe are in reality financed by European holdings of dollars. He has asked me to

comment on this question in the light of President de
Gaulle's statement of February 1965 on gold and dollars, and the sentiments against American investments
increasingly expressed by Europeans, as, for example,
by Hermann J. Abs, the President of the Deutsche Bank
of Frankfurt. For what they may be worth I am pleased
to offer some summary remarks on these complex issues
as a supplement to his study in depth.

In my judgment, there is a serious confusion among
Americans and Europeans alike between direct investment on the one hand and liquidity investment on the
other. Direct investment is possible because American
companies can earn a higher return in, say, France not
only than they can earn in the United States, but higher
than French companies can earn in France. The reason
for these higher earnings is that they have a monopoly
advantage over French companies; that is, they can do
something the French companies cannot do. It is of
profound significance that while the French authorities
expressed great concern over the establishment of a
canning plant by Libby, McNeill & Libby or the purchase of Machines Bull in computers by the General
Electric Company, in each case, after the facts had been
examined, the investment was allowed to go through.
The American company had a useful contribution to
make in breaking economic bottlenecks in France. The
remedy for monopoly is not less output but more. If *The
New York Times* is to be believed, moreover, the French
government actively sought to attract to Strasbourg the
General Motors plant which is settling in Antwerp. It
is one thing to fulminate against American investment

in general on nationalistic political grounds; it is something else again to give up the productive and technical advantages which such investment offers.

One of the French points against United States investment, as Mr. Johnstone fully expounds, is that capital controls are used to implement French planning, and that foreign corporations with funds from abroad can escape capital controls and thus frustrate planning. But in the Libby, McNeill & Libby case, in General Motors at Antwerp, and in countless other cases, the United States firm puts up a minimum of its own funds and borrows to the maximum in the local money and capital markets. It submits to local capital controls. An American concern in France will be financed with French monies, to be sure, but not through the balance-of-payments mechanism, of which so much is made: France holding dollars in New York to enable American companies to acquire bricks and mortar and machines in France.

The European acquisitions of dollars, in my view, have a rather different purpose than financing take-overs of European firms by United States capital. Until the interest-equalization tax, the Gore amendment, and in March 1965 the President's program of voluntary controls on new investments abroad, a very considerable part of the increase in European cash in New York was the result of an exchange of cash against long-term borrowing. European savers who were unable to find short-term assets in their own money markets had to go abroad; at the same time, European borrowers who were unable to make long-term commitments in their own capital market could obtain long-term credit in the Euro-dollar market and in New York with investment houses or banks. What was taking place, as I see it, was an international bargain in liquidity: European money and capital markets traded increased liquidity for savers and illiquidity for firms undertaking investment against the difference between the two rates of interest. European holdings of dollars financed not United States direct investment so much as European borrowings of dollars on long-term account. This came about in the normal economic way: because of differences in interest rates, which, on long-term account, were much higher in Europe than in the United States.

It will be some time, I believe, before this analysis of the problem of United States–European balances of payments is accepted. The issues will become clearer as the cutting off of United States investment in United States dollar bonds, bank loans, and loans through the Euro-dollar market leads to tightened interest rates in Europe and difficulties for firms trying to borrow for investment. In the meantime, while analysts are focusing on the direct-investment issue, Allan W. Johnstone's Master's thesis makes a cool, competent, and insightful contribution to the discussion.

C. P. KINDLEBERGER
Professor of Economics
Massachusetts Institute of Technology

March 1965

Author's Preface

United States direct investment in Western Europe has never been of greater concern to Europeans than it is today. Virtually every major American investment sets off a new public outcry. Recurrent newspaper articles continue to draw wide attention to the latest acquisition or joint venture and bring forth an outpouring of critical comment from every quarter.

Nowhere in Europe have American investors provoked more reaction, or encountered a cooler reception, than in France. The latest move in what often appears to be a campaign against foreign investors appeared in the form of a report issued by the Patronat, France's influential association of manufacturers. Their report, comparing French companies to the largest American and British firms, ranks the largest French company only fifty-seventh in the listing, based upon annual sales. Ten French companies—as against 114 American— were shown to have a yearly turnover of more than $500 million. The inferences and conclusions are clear to the reader and seem intended solely to rally new support for the contention that French business needs protection from United States competition.

Because of this continuing controversy and the involvement of my own company in it, I have observed each new development with intense interest. As a Fellow at the Alfred P. Sloan School of Management at M.I.T., on leave from Chrysler International S.A. for a year of study, I was given an opportunity to write a thesis on a subject of my choice. I chose to investigate the French claims that U.S. investment presents a threat to economic sovereignty; this book is the result of my research. If it produces nothing more in the reader than a new appreciation of the French point of view, its publication will have served a useful purpose.

It would be appropriate here to acknowledge the guidance and encouragement given me throughout my endeavors by Professor Charles P. Kindleberger and Dr. Richard D. Robinson, of the faculty of the Massachusetts Institute of Technology. I am mindful also of my debt to the many anonymous business executives who generously contributed time to discussions of which I was the sole beneficiary. To all those who lent assistance, I am sincerely grateful.

ALLAN W. JOHNSTONE

Geneva, Switzerland
November 1964

Contents

United States
Direct Investment in France

CHAPTER ONE

Introduction

Le grand commerce est le moyen d'augmenter la puissance et la grandeur de sa Majesté et d'abaisser celles de ses ennemis et envieux.

Jean-Baptiste Colbert,
French Financier, 1619–1683

The attitude of the French government toward U.S. direct investment in France, as officially expressed, has undergone a fundamental change during recent years. Long welcomed as palliation of chronic capital shortages and dollar deficits, U.S. direct investment in that country has come under intense scrutiny since August, 1962, in an atmosphere increasingly inhospitable to any further extension of American economic influence. The concern of France has been manifested not only in the candid admissions of the highest government officials but in proposals to her fellow-member states within the European Economic Community as well, urging upon them proposals for the collective control of foreign investment.

French fears, or at least those which have been publicly articulated, are grounded in four main postulates.

The first of these is the belief that American investors exercise excessive external management control of their French subsidiaries and branches. Second, the French argue that such external control is often exercised in ways inimical to legitimate French national interests. Third, they aver that certain key industries are either already under foreign control, or in imminent danger of the heavy concentration of foreign capital in those industries. And finally, French critics state that United States or other foreign control tends to remove an industry or, indeed, an entire sector of the economy from the reaches of the national economic planning mechanism. Other fears have been voiced, but none so plainly as these.

PURPOSE OF THE STUDY

The purpose of the study is to weigh the evidence supporting these French beliefs and, from the conclusions thus reached, to anticipate the future policies of the French government concerning U.S. direct investment. In accomplishing this purpose, it is the task of the study (1) to review the events which have provoked French reaction; (2) to characterize French attitudes toward U.S. investment; (3) to examine the dimensions of U.S. direct investment in France; (4) to determine which policies are typically reserved to the parent company for decision and which are left to the subsidiary for autonomous determination; and (5) to gauge the vulnerability of foreign investors to new regulation by French governmental authority.

The book draws upon a careful survey of the control policies and practices followed by twenty-four large American companies with subsidiaries in France, as well as upon the published materials. By relating the underlying issue of control to a consideration of the other aspects of the problem, the discussion has been designed to improve understanding of Gallic attitudes and of France's capability to regulate U.S. investment in that country.

LIMITATIONS OF THE STUDY

It should be observed at the outset that the study confines itself exclusively to U.S. direct private investment. This investment, as distinguished from portfolio investment, is the equity held by U.S. investors in French business enterprise acquired for the purpose of influencing or controlling the activities of that enterprise. As defined by the Office of Business Economics, U.S. Department of Commerce, for statistical use, it does not include miscellaneous holdings of stocks and bonds of foreign issuers. It is not only the equity in corporations, but also the investment in sole proprietorships and partnerships held by residents of the United States. French attention has been focused primarily upon direct, rather than portfolio, investment.

The study is unquestionably colored by the range and scope of the survey upon which certain conclusions concerning the nature of control exercised are based. Because interviews were conducted in only twenty-four of an estimated four hundred U.S. firms with operating subsidiaries or branches in France,[1] the findings presented must be qualified. While the author believes that the practices followed by the companies interviewed are widely observed, he cannot preclude, on the basis of evidence submitted, the existence of other parent companies which wield far greater influence in the affairs of their French subsidiaries than those included in this investigation. The survey taken has, in fact, revealed a broad variance in matters over which control is exerted and the degree to which it is exercised. The study is not offered as absolute evidence in support of any premise that *most* parent companies exercise too much or too little control of French subsidiaries, but only as an indication of the extent and nature of control as exercised by *some* companies. The author also recognizes that practices may vary from industry to industry as well as from company to company. No attempt is made to discern whether bias exists in these findings, as a result.

The study is further limited. The French allegation that French subsidiaries of U.S. companies are often managed in disregard of the interests of the host country and to the detriment of France cannot properly be judged from data available to the student in this country. Only a thorough investigation in France would disclose whether "misconduct" is widespread, and whether actions of American investors do constitute a threat to

---

[1] According to the *Alphabetical Listing of Subsidiaries and Branches of U.S. Firms Operating in France*, compiled by the Office of the Counselor of Embassy for Commercial Affairs, Embassy of the United States in Paris, there were 395 such firms as of November 15, 1963.

the socioeconomic objectives of the French nation. There has been far more misinformation published on this aspect of the problem, even in the French press, than there have been facts brought to light. This question is deserving of additional attention.

A final caveat remains. The point of view expressed by the respondents interviewed throughout the survey was that of an executive of the parent company, speaking usually as the superior of the senior executive of the French subsidiary. The respondent was invariably an American, who often had a wealth of international business experience but who generally had not served his company in France as its local manager. It is conceivable, therefore, that a survey taken in France of the impressions of the responsible local executives would reveal a different pattern of response. It is also very probable that interviews conducted in France would disclose broader differences in opinion concerning the desirability of control than in the ways in which parent companies seek to exercise it.

PREVIOUS INVESTIGATIONS

Little has been written concerning the means by which operating control is exercised by a parent company of its foreign subsidiary.[2] While there are many oblique references to problems of operating control in the growing body of literature used to familiarize the business

[2] The only such publication is a case study prepared under the auspices of the National Planning Association: Boyd France, *The Case Study of IBM in France, Studies in United States Business Performance Abroad* (Washington, D. C.: National Planning Association, 1961), 85 pp.

school student with international business management, the only published materials that deal specifically with this subject are those of the International Management Association, Inc. A series of five case studies contributed by members of the association were grouped in a single publication[3] in 1957. Two similar and related reports have been issued since then.[4]

These investigations provide useful knowledge relative to the need for, and desirability of, control as well as the means by which it is exerted. The published findings are briefly reviewed in Chapter 5, supplementing the data obtained in the survey.

There is also a remarkable dearth of documentation upon all other aspects of the problems considered in this study. Only two works which deal directly and comprehensively with the subject have been published, and both are in French.[5] This lack of published materials handicaps the student who would seek a diversity of opinion.

ORGANIZATION OF THE STUDY

The recent history of events in France which have led to proposals for stringent control of foreign inves-

[3] *Case Studies in Foreign Operations, IMA Special Report No. 1* (New York: American Management Association, Inc., 1957), 237 pp.

[4] L. Kamsky and others, *Applying Financial Controls in Foreign Operations, IMA Special Report No. 2* and *Increasing Profits from Foreign Operations, IMA Special Report No. 3* (New York: American Management Association, Inc., 1957), 177 pp. and 240 pp., respectively.

[5] Gilles-Y. Bertin, *L'Investissement des Firmes Étrangères en France* (Paris: Presses Universitaires de France, 1963), 324 pp.; Jacques Gervais, *La France Face aux Investissements Étrangers* (Paris: Editions de l'Entreprise Moderne, 1963), 235 pp.

tors is reviewed in detail in Chapter 2. The actions of the companies involved are put in chronological perspective together with the gathering storm of reaction in the French ministries to which protests were directed.

In Chapter 3 is described the complex of fears and anxieties which have shaped French attitudes toward the events related in the foregoing pages and which will guide the hand of government in future dealings with foreign investors.

Chapter 4 contains relevant data depicting the size and scope of United States direct investment in France. It delineates not only the volume of investment and the trend of growth but also the role of American investment in, and its contribution to, the French economy. American investor participation in selected industries is described to permit evaluation of the charge that U.S. investment has been concentrated in several narrow, key sectors of industry.

The findings of the survey, aimed at a determination of the extent and degree of control exercised by parent companies, are set forth in Chapter 5. Following an explanation of the methodology used in the selection of respondents and the conduct of interviews is a full account of the information gleaned from the interviews. Techniques of control commonly used are identified, policies reserved for parent determination are differentiated from those in which the subordinate organization acts with full autonomy, and an attempt is made to characterize the extent and degree of external management control typical of the twenty-four respondent companies. A final section of the chapter deals with replies to questions posed during the interview which were intended to elicit evidence of discrimination toward U.S. investors.

Discussed in broad terms in Chapter 6 is the vulnerability of U.S. investors to restrictive regulatory action by the French government. Taking note of French proposals to curb United States and other foreign investment, the writer cites the legal disabilities and other considerations inhibiting France from acting unilaterally.

In the last chapter, the material presented in preceding chapters is summarized. The more important findings of the study are outlined, and certain conclusions are drawn from the investigation. The book concludes with a recommendation for additional research beyond the limits of the undertaking reported.

SOURCES OF DATA

For the historical résumé and review of developments culminating in French official reaction and for the current status of the problem, the writer has relied heavily upon articles appearing in both French and American periodicals. Several interviews divulged additional useful information pertinent to events which occurred in France when French apprehension seemed most acute. Material for the chapter on the size and scope of U.S. investment in France came from a variety of sources, including reports of the U.S. Department of Commerce and the permanent French and American literature on the subject. The survey data is the contribution of key executives in twenty-four large American companies, all competent to answer in the matter under discussion and willing to provide the information. For the knowledge imparted in the chapter on vulnerability to regulation, the writer has resorted to the American literature covering the applicable laws.

Supplementing the foregoing sources were additional interviews conducted in three major American banking firms with branches in Paris. The writer has also been given fortunate access to members of the American diplomatic staff who are intimately familiar with recent developments and who have supplied much unpublished information.

CHAPTER TWO

A Chronicle of Events Provoking a Change in Policy

To understand the demands emanating from France that member nations of the European Economic Community adopt some form of control of foreign, that is, non-EEC, investment within the community, it is necessary to view retrospectively the sequence of events in France which excited national attention. Accordingly, a full and particular account of the brief history of the affair, as it was reported in current American and French newspapers and periodicals, is given here. By their actions, four American companies appear to have provoked the outpouring of criticism. Through a review of the part each played and significant developments since then, it is possible to discern a change in French policy concerning new foreign investment.

GENERAL MOTORS AND REMINGTON RAND ANNOUNCE MASS LAYOFFS

On August 31, 1962, General Motors France, the country's largest refrigerator manufacturer, served notice of discharge upon 685 of its 3,100 employees at the Frigidaire plant in the Paris suburb of Gennevilliers. The 685 workmen, who individually had received no warning that their jobs were in jeopardy, included nine union representatives. Some hours later, the two trade unions represented in the plant (the communist-dominated Confédération Générale du Travail and the Roman Catholic Confédération Française des Travailleurs Chrétiens) united to stage a protest demonstration in front of the company offices. General Motors spokesmen refused to reconsider the decision, justifying their action as a simple reaction to new conditions brought about by the lowered internal tariffs of the EEC. They said General Motors had sustained the loss of a sizable share of its market, as had other refrigerator producers in France, when large numbers of low-priced Italian-made refrigerators were offered for sale. The massive imports of Italian units had necessitated a curtailment of more than 20 per cent of the work force.[1]

Ten days later the subsidiary of another American company, Remington Rand France, announced that during the following four months it would dismiss 800 of the 1,200 workers employed at Caluire-et-Cuire, near Lyon. Manufacture of office equipment would continue in the existing facility, but production of portable typewriters was to be concentrated in a more modern plant in Holland because of declining sales both in France and the United States.[2] Remington's public an-

---

[1] A number of periodicals carried accounts of the General Motors case. The best appeared in *The Reporter*, June 6, 1963, p. 23.

[2] News item in *Business Week*, September 22, 1962, p. 96.

nouncement was the first knowledge government officials had of the company's intention to curtail employment and close down typewriter operations. Trade union representatives, again aroused, seized upon this second reduction in the work force of an American-owned company to lodge a complaint with the Ministry of Industry and Commerce. The charge was made and not denied that the decision to fire the Remington workers was sent by teletype from the United States.

Responding on September 14 to the dissatisfaction expressed by the unions and echoed in the French press, Minister of Industry Michel Maurice-Bokanowski issued a public denunciation. He would not permit, he said, "certain isolated enterprises to practice an irresponsible policy that does not respect the social contract linking a financially powerful enterprise to the labor it employs." Minister Maurice-Bokanowski added that the government was planning to establish special regulations covering foreign investments in France, and would seek to impose the requirement that foreign-controlled companies henceforth consult with affected ministries of the government in Paris before dismissing redundant employees. He added ominously, "In the future new foreign investment programs, particularly from U.S. firms, must be examined with greatest care."[3]

Both companies disclaimed the charge of irresponsibility. General Motors officials averred that the required notification had been served upon the government advising the Ministry of Labor of the impending layoff.

[3] Quoted in *Time*, September 21, 1962, p. 88.

They complained that other French refrigerator producers had also cut back their employment without the recriminations attending the General Motors action. They also noted that General Motors had taken the lead, in the face of French skepticism, in establishing the refrigerator industry in France after World War II. By 1962 it had become France's leading refrigerator manufacturer, and, therefore, attracted more attention than its smaller French competitors.

Remington's reply to the press laid stress upon the undisputed fact that there was a severe labor shortage in much of France, and new jobs were easily to be secured. Hopeful of avoiding the unfavorable publicity which General Motors had suffered, Remington officials pointed out that the company had assisted 80 per cent of the discharged workers to find new employment. It charged that the French government was at least partly responsible for the shutdown, having recently bought cheaper West German models in preference to the French-made Remington machines. By February, 1963, Remington had dismissed its entire work force, transferring its operations to other plants in Holland and West Germany.

Inasmuch as it was admitted that job opportunities were abundant, and that, in any case, the number of workers affected in the two incidents was hardly large enough to affect the regional, let alone the national, economic situation, press observers looked for other more plausible reasons for the French outburst. Explanation was thought to lie in the timing of the two companies' announcements, which were made when government officials were conferring with representatives of unions and employers on wage policy matters. The annoyance of Maurice-Bokanowski stemmed at least partly from his feeling that if the companies had warned him sufficiently in advance, he might have been able to give special assistance to the firms, avoiding the necessity of a layoff.

An even more persuasive reason which was given concerned the French attitude toward job mobility and the employment relationship. The belief is widespread in France that the burden of adjusting to changing market conditions is one which should be borne by the employer and one seldom, if ever, to be shared by the work force. Many thought this to be the true reason for dissatisfaction.

CHRYSLER CORPORATION ACQUIRES MAJORITY CONTROL OF SIMCA

Four days after President Charles de Gaulle vetoed Britain's entry into the EEC for, among many reasons, the "undesirability of Anglo-American economic influence," Chrysler Corporation issued a press release stating that it had increased its interest in Simca from 25 to 63.8 per cent by buying an additional block of shares. With 63 per cent of total equity, representing an investment exceeding $130 million, Chrysler had acquired majority control of France's third largest automobile producer and fifth ranking industrial company, according to volume of sales. Through Swiss banks it had purchased shares held by other investors outside of France.[4]

On the following day, January 19, 1963, the Ministry of Finance made a public statement calling for restrictions upon investment from outside the EEC, and proposing consideration of the problem at the then forthcoming meeting of the six EEC finance ministers on January 31 at Baden-Baden, West Germany. In the days ensuing, several prominent government officials, among them Premier Georges Pompidou and Minister of Finance, Valéry Giscard d'Estaing, voiced concern. Premier Pompidou told an American Chamber of Commerce audience that "United States investments in France constitute an essentially healthy phenomenon the consequences of which must, however, be studied. . . . We must take account of the size of the respective economies and of our concern over planning."[5] The Finance Minister spoke more bluntly a week later: "It is not desirable that important sectors of the Common Market's economy depend on outside decisions."[6]

In the furore that arose over the Chrysler affair, the French officials neglected to take cognizance of two important facts. First, Simca had long been controlled by interests outside of France; second, the transfer involved was one between a foreign corporation and other foreign shareholders. The communiqué released by the

[4] This episode is well reported in *Business Week*, January 26, 1963, p. 100.
[5] Quoted in *Business International*, February 1, 1963, p. 1. (Weekly newsletter to members.)
[6] Quoted in *Time*, February 1, 1963, p. 43.

Ministry of Finance said only that Chrysler's move was "an intervention in a particularly important branch of European industry in which participation from the outside is already considerable." The government regarded it simply as "a new example of the problems posed by foreign investment."

THE LIBBY, McNEILL & LIBBY PROPOSALS ARE PUBLICIZED

In the edition of January 25, one week after the Chrysler announcement had refueled the controversy which began with the General Motors and Remington cases in September, *Le Monde*, the influential Paris newspaper, carried news of a Libby, McNeill & Libby proposal to build a $6.5 million cannery in the Bas-Rhône-Languedoc region.[7] Initial output was planned for 200,000 tons annually, with processing to begin in 1967. The story, which set off a barrage of protests, was leaked, presumably by someone in the government. The company denied releasing it.

Libby's interest in France dated back to 1961, when company officials first learned of the vast irrigation project undertaken by the government in Southeastern France. Encouraged by influential French business interests favoring a large American food-processing establishment to support the agricultural development of the area, Libby began negotiations with the Ministry of Agriculture and the Ministry of Finance. By early January, 1963, tentative agreement had been reached upon

[7] News item in *Le Monde*, January 25, 1963, p. 14.

Libby's investment application. Top officials of both ministries had assured Libby that formal approval would be forthcoming later that month. They advised the company that it could make the investment without any restriction providing for French equity participation. The government, they said, would release a communiqué to the press later in the month.

Libby officials insisted that its proposal was leaked, for political reasons, on the eve of the Baden-Baden conference. The French press intensified its attack, citing as bases for objection the massive importation of U.S. produce (adding to the burden of France's own agricultural surpluses), the laws enacted in July, 1962, forbidding vertical integration by food-processing companies, and potential noncompliance with price regulation. The charges made in the newspapers were either untrue or inapplicable to the Libby case and only further inflamed French opinion.

The true explanation was to be found elsewhere. France had already spent $160 million to rehabilitate 250,000 hectares (over half a million acres) of land in this region in order to encourage vegetable and fruit growers to join with French canners in establishing a major canning industry there. The nearly one thousand small and inefficient canning companies of France, all of which had ignored the incentives placed before them by the government, feared the Libby proposal. The prospect that a large American enterprise might become the primary beneficiary of a state investment enraged many French people.[8]

8 See *The Reporter*, June 6, 1963, p. 25.

*FRANCE FAILS TO ENLIST SUPPORT
WITHIN THE EEC*

The meeting of the finance ministers of the Common Market scheduled for February 1 was called off when France's five partners unceremoniously declined to appear. In the frigid aftermath of de Gaulle's veto, none of the other members of the EEC desired to consider the matter, as proposed. The meeting was rescheduled and again postponed, but finally did convene on March 27, 1963.

The reaction of the finance ministers, as reported in the press dispatches, evidenced no sympathy for the French insistence upon a plan to curb United States investment within the borders of the EEC. The only agreement on this question was reached on a proposal by French Minister d'Estaing that each member supply the EEC Executive Commission with figures on third-country investment in member nations, and that the Commission collate and publish these figures. The French minister also suggested that an industry-by-industry report showing the extent of foreign penetration in the EEC be presented at the finance ministers' next meeting in June. The West German and Italian ministers stated their governments' friendly attitude toward U.S. investors. They argued that any measures designed to block foreign investors ran counter to the freedom of capital movement to which each member nation was bound by the Treaty of Rome. The issue was tabled; a report would be issued quietly at a later date.[9]

9 News item in *Newsweek*, April 8, 1963, p. 68.

A publication prepared by the EEC commission on the very subject of American investment in Europe had actually been circulated in advance of the March meeting. The data were gathered principally from U.S. government publications. It showed that total investment expenditure from all sources by U.S. investors amounted to approximately 2 per cent of gross capital formation in the six-nation EEC. France had the lowest percentage of U.S.-controlled investment, with 1.4 per cent. Highest was Germany, with 3.1 per cent.[10]

These figures, which were internationally publicized, tranquilized the French press. As one writer has noted, "It was hard to see as the ogre a foreign group controlling only 1.4 per cent of French investment or, alternatively, as the friendly giant whose picture had been drawn by some in public debate." Whatever their effect, no further effort was made at the following meeting, on June 7, to obtain agreement on restrictions of third-country capital investment in the EEC. Later events revealed that a change in investment policy had occurred, however, one which the French government would implement unilaterally.

FOREIGN INVESTMENT POLICY PRIOR TO 1963

To understand what change in policy had taken place it is necessary to know what the attitude of the government had been. Prior to World War II, the French government imposed no restrictions upon the inflow of private foreign investment, either direct or portfolio.

[10] Item in *Business International,* March 29, 1963, p. 7.

During the postwar period, the government began to control all international financial transactions and capital movements. Imports of foreign capital were encouraged as contributions to France's meager foreign exchange reserves.

The government actively sought after 1946 to foster virtually all kinds of foreign investment, particularly American, in French industry. It was only moderately successful until the Common Market was formed. Between March, 1957, the start of the Common Market, and February, 1963, some 345 new U.S. companies established operations in France.

From time to time, however, the French government delayed and discouraged foreign investors through the screening process, the system of prior authorization that had to be obtained in order to repatriate capital or profits. This was thought to reflect the pressures on the government from French businessmen who feared potential competition from American firms seeking to migrate to France. Notwithstanding this opposition, the determined U.S. company in an industry open to foreign investment was always able to enter; during the period 1957–1962 there was no single known instance in which the French permanently blocked an investment.

No criteria were published whereby the investor could determine in advance whether his investment proposal met the standard set by French policy.[11] Foreign investors were required to file a comprehensive application with the Ministry of Finance, where an attempt was

11 *Business Operations in France, A Guide for American Investors* (Washington, D. C.: Comité Franc-Dollar, 1961), pp. 4–5.

made to fit new investments into the general pattern
of the country's economic development. The Ministry
of Finance reviewed each investment application on its
merits, calling for advisory opinions from the Ministry
of Industry. Investments that would facilitate the expansion of insufficiently developed segments of the
economy, or those undertakings that would contribute
to the improvements of France's balance-of-payments
position, were looked upon with especial favor. There
were no prescribed conditions which, when met, auto-
matically assured approval of an investment.

A NEW POLICY BECOMES APPARENT THROUGH GOVERNMENT ACTION

Following the crisis created by General Motors and
Remington and exacerbated by the actions of Chrysler
and Libby, the government, which had given prelimi-
nary approval, suspended further action on the Libby
application. Libby executives who inquired concerning
the application were told that approval could be given
only if the company were willing to yield part ownership
of the parent company to French investors. As proof of
its intention, the government offered to bring Libby together with interested local investors. Libby agreed, and
four months later 20 per cent of the outstanding equity
had been transferred to a French investment company.[12]
By July, 1963, 40 per cent of the shares in Libby, representing effective control of the company, were in the
possession of European investors. Libby's eighteen-
month-old application now presented no difficulty.

[12] Item in *Business International*, May 17, 1963, p. 2.

A second significant application was submitted by General Electric Company to the Ministry of Finance in 1963. Machines Bull, a French manufacturer of computers and data processing machines, had fallen into financial difficulty, and urgently needed a large infusion of new capital funds; General Electric had offered to purchase as much as 20 per cent of Bull's shares, and provide the urgently needed funds.[13] The General Electric application was first rejected on February 6, 1964.[14]

The reason for rejection was given in a public statement by the Ministry of Finance. The government, it said, "couldn't agree to the prospective acquisition of a part of [Bull's] capital by a foreign company." It had earlier noted that the only other computer manufacturer, IBM of France, was a wholly owned U.S. company which accounted for almost 50 per cent of computer output.

At the urging of the government, Bull thereafter sought and received financial backing from French banking and industrial sources. This aid offered only short-term relief, however, and Bull and General Electric negotiators made a second attempt to overcome French objections, which stemmed from the unwillingness of the government to give to a foreign investor the controlling voice in the only truly French company in an industry essential to the nation's defense.

The persistence of the negotiators was ultimately rewarded when, in mid-July, executives of the two firms

---

[13] Article in *Business Week*, January 25, 1964, pp. 58–60.
[14] News item in *The Wall Street Journal*, February 6, 1964, p. 4.

jubilantly announced[15] that agreement had been reached upon a joint venture which had been "designed with a view toward meeting the concerns voiced by the government." Under the agreement, Compagnie des Machines Bull was to be reorganized as a holding company with three subsidiaries created to handle the activities of the old company. For $43 million General Electric would obtain 49 per cent of the computer manufacturing and research subsidiary, 49 per cent of the subsidiary conducting market research and development work in France, and 51 per cent of the subsidiary responsible for worldwide marketing. In each company, Bull retained the remaining interest. A fourth company, separate and entirely French-owned, will carry on defense work of a classified nature. The solution finally reached was said to have the official approval, if not the blessing, of President Charles de Gaulle.

From the Libby and General Electric cases, it became evident that the French government was enforcing a new policy. It would not permit control of an industry to fall into the hands of foreign investors, nor would it allow any single foreign company to establish itself as a dominant force in any region of the country.

THE RATIONALE BEHIND FRENCH POLICY

American investment in France, as will be seen in the next chapter, has expanded rapidly since 1957, troubling many Frenchmen. Also alarming from the French point of view was the heavy concentration of U.S. in-

[15] News item in *The Wall Street Journal*, July 24, 1964, p. 4.

vestment in certain key industries. The carbon black industry, indispensable to the manufacture of rubber, is comprised, for example, of three companies all of which are subsidiaries of U.S. parent companies.

The attitude of the French government toward this state of affairs was succinctly summarized on May 27, 1963, by Premier Pompidou. He said:

France is not hostile to foreign investments: however, a limitation appears desirable in practice. France does not wish that the industry of a particular region or a particular branch of industry be dominated by foreign capital, for example, American. Hence, the government favors a control which would prevent the development of such monopolies, this being true not only for American capital but for all foreign capital except that of the Six for which there exists complete freedom of movement.[16]

Another French official, Ambassador to the United States Hervé Alphand, spoke on the subject on September 25, in Washington, D. C. He phrased it this way:

We must, as must other countries of the world, supervise the total of investments coming from abroad. It is true that it is not possible for us to leave certain sectors of our economy, certain of our large enterprises, in the hands of companies whose head offices are in Chicago or Detroit. But it is not true that we do not accept with pleasure in the great majority of cases — in fact, we have never rejected them — all American investment which may certainly constitute a large complement and a large stimulant for our policy of expansion in France.

[16] Spoken at a reception for fifty representatives of large international firms in Paris; quoted in the *Economic Summary — Second Quarter, 1963* (unpublished communication from Counselor for Commercial Affairs, U.S. Embassy, Paris, to the Department of State, August 15, 1963), p. 7.

The legend of a France which forbids the investments of American capital in the French economy is entirely false.[17]

From the two statements (and the earlier statement by Pompidou on January 23), the salient features of the new policy could easily have been identified. France would no longer allow dominant control of an industry, or even a large company within it, to come within the province of a foreign investor; it wished to supervise foreign investors; and it would permit new investment only if it complemented the French economy, and stimulated expansion. Although control of foreign investment already within France was not specifically mentioned, these statements, taken in the context of others like those of Maurice-Bokanowski, left little doubt that the government was considering some form of regulation of the actions of foreign investors already doing business in France.

[17] Quoted in the *Economic Summary — Third Quarter, 1963* (unpublished communication from Counselor for Commercial Affairs, U.S. Embassy, Paris, to the Department of State, October 30, 1963), p. 9.

CHAPTER THREE

French Fears and Apprehensions

Behind the official pronouncements lie a complex of apprehensions that furnished critics of U.S. investment with support from widely divergent elements of French society. The veritable barrage of unfavorable publicity attending the events described in the preceding chapter brought to the surface of public awareness many fears or feelings of anxiety. These fears, held by Frenchmen of every persuasion, could not be lightly dismissed as evidence of the cultural ethnocentricity of which the French are so often accused. Some familiarity with the beliefs nurturing mistrust is a prerequisite to a thorough understanding of the subject; these beliefs are, therefore, given cursory examination in this chapter.

OFFICIAL CONCERNS

Official misgivings result from the belief of many administrators, already mentioned, that foreign control of certain industrial sectors may interfere with the execution of economic policy. Concern has been expressed that unrestricted investment would hamper the government in the exercise of its economic planning function and that uncontrolled investment could have deleterious effects upon the balance of payments.

The Threat to Economic Planning

The goal of "indicative planning," as economic planning is called in France, is the improvement of productive efficiency and social welfare without recourse to authoritarian control (*dirigisme*). National economic planning, as carried out by the French Commissariat Général au Plan, depends in considerable measure for its success upon the extent of cooperation it receives from private industry. In the case of many French-owned companies, cooperation has been secured by granting or withholding credit.[1]

This use of credit as an instrument of control is highly effective in France, which has no market for long-term capital, except at comparatively high interest rates, and only a weak capital market for short- and medium-term credits. State funds are loaned to cure this deficiency, and government intervention has made possible many important capital investment on terms which could not have been obtained otherwise. Long-term low-interest loans, tax relief, and outright grants have all been used to entice participation by industries.

Under French banking regulations, all medium- and long-term credit of more than two years is centrally controlled by the government and by quasi-governmen-

[1] John Sheahan, *Promotion and Control of Industry in Postwar France* (Cambridge, Mass.: Harvard University Press, 1963), p. 32.

tal institutions such as the Banque de France, Crédit National, Crédit Foncier, and the Fonds de Développement Économique et Social. Credit controls are comprehensive, applying even to short-term financing in which a company borrowing more than the equivalent of $2 million must have specific approval from the Banque de France. With foreign companies, particularly those based in the United States, circumvention of control is often easy; access to bank financing, a great advantage for most French firms, is a less powerful lever of influence.[2]

Proponents of active planning who attribute economic growth in France to the four-year plans resent the freedom thus open to subsidiaries of foreign companies. When firms have acted independently, their actions have been interpreted as another form of refusal to cooperate, diverting resources away from planned objectives, and making results differ from collective goals. American enterprise, known universally for its ardent faith in competition and distaste for governmental control, cannot, in the opinion of many Frenchmen, be relied upon to cooperate.

Spokesman for those who share this fear is Pierre Massé, present head of the Commissariat au Plan. Massé has written, "I readily concede the tonic value of competition, but it is essential to be able to recognize the dividing line between incentive and waste, especially where costly investments and risks of underemployment

[2] John Hackett and Anne-Marie Hackett, *Economic Planning in France* (London: G. Allen & Unwin, 1963), p. 267.

are involved."[3] Massé makes oblique reference in his
statement to two other fears, namely, those of overcapacity and of resultant unemployment. In doing so, he
might well have had in mind U.S. participation in the
European automobile industry, which is often cited as
the outstanding example of overcapacity.

American automobile companies produce 30 per cent
of German-built vehicles and 40 per cent of the automobiles made in Britain. The Ford Motor Company has
already invested in Europe three times the capital invested by Renault in France, and continues to expand
its production capacity in England, Belgium, and Germany. When economists compare projected capacity in
1966 of seven million vehicles with market estimates of
six million units, including exports, they wonder at the
consequences. They fear that in any future test of
strength the vastly stronger American companies will
prevail.[4] European firms as a result will be driven out
of business, their plants closed, and workers idled. The
perturbations would be felt not only by those directly
interested in the manufacture of motor vehicles but by
those in support industries as well.

The Sensitive Industries

Although the French government has not yet drawn
official guidelines designating those industries in which
it would welcome or turn away new U.S. investment, it

[3] From "French Planning," *French Affairs,* No. 127, December, 1961,
quoted in John Sheahan, *Promotion and Control of Industry in Postwar
France, op. cit.,* p. 183 f.
[4] "French Motors — Manufacturers on Their Guard," *Economist, 207*:
273, April 20, 1963.

is clear that there are three industries which it considers "sensitive." It has shown unusual concern for investment applications by companies in the automotive, food, and electronics fields. The European automobile industry, dominated as it is already by U.S. companies, has such influence over the economy that another takeover attempt would certainly meet with opposition. The active search by a number of large U.S. food companies for company acquisitions in France has alarmed the government to the possibility of foreign dominance in a field in which the French are notoriously inefficient. Finally, the French are reluctant to become too dependent upon U.S. companies for electronics development because of its importance to the military defense effort. As seen in the previous chapter, the French government recently prevented an American company from acquiring control of Machines Bull, a large supplier of electronic equipment for military use. One of the important reasons for the government's insistence that the data processing research and development activity be controlled by Bull was its feeling that such work would otherwise be carried out in the United States, with no technological fallout accruing to France.

It must be added that the petroleum industry, in which the government itself has important financial interests, is also sensitive. Prompted by the discovery of vast oil reserves in the French Sahara, the government moved to limit foreign participation in this industry in 1959, when it formed the Union Industrielle des Pétroles. In exchange for 40 per cent of the shares, Caltex, an important U.S. oil company, was induced to convey its entire assets, including a large Bordeaux refinery, to the government-controlled company.

Governmental quota regulations promulgated in 1963 will limit crude-oil imports from outside the franc zone by foreign-owned oil companies during a ten-year period beginning in 1965. These regulations are intended to increase the reliance of foreign oil companies upon the higher-cost crude from the Sahara oil fields. To confer even greater advantage upon Union Générale des Pétroles, the new state oil company, the government allocated to it 14.5 per cent of the total quota for crude oil originating outside the franc zone. In 1964 the government announced that no new retail gasoline outlets could be built without official authorization.[5] The latest decree, challenged by the international companies, has been upheld by the government.

Balance of Payments Considerations

The long-range effect of the inflow of capital investment on the French balance of payments also causes some anxiety. Although new foreign investment is approved, presumably, only when it may be shown that the investment will create net exports, reduce essential imports, and save foreign exchange through the production in France of items that would otherwise have to be imported, there are economists who fear potential repercussions in a period of crisis or of prolonged business recession.[6] Memories of the early postwar years when

[5] "France Adds Muscle to State Oil Companies by Curbing Its International Rivals," *Business Week*, July 4, 1964, p. 78.

[6] Bertin, *op. cit.*, pp. 262–277.

chronic dollar deficits spawned a web of currency regulations remain vivid in some minds. The possibility that dividends or other capital transfers abroad after a period of time could exceed the annual inflow of initially invested capital has troubled still others.[7] Exchange controls, as applied in France, have never limited dividends as such to a proportion of capital invested. Few companies have repatriated exorbitant shares of initial capital or retained earnings, but the absence of control could result in a heavy drain over the short term, tending to upset a favorable balance of payments.

In the past, the government has been forced to control all international financial transactions in order to prevent the flight of French capital and depletion of meager foreign currency reserves. Since the initiation of the franc stabilization program in 1958 and the return to convertibility on current account, there has been, however, complete relaxation of control.

POPULAR FEARS

Certain prevalent attitudes toward competition, toward U.S. enterprise, and toward foreign influence whatever its origin have contributed to the anxiety of many people outside the government community.

Attitudes Toward Competition

Opposition to private foreign investment is a natural reaction of French businessmen when confronted by

[7] Gervais, *op. cit.*, pp. 174–175.

competition from foreign financial rivals in the local markets, especially large and powerful rivals. France, which is still a nation of small shopkeepers, has long been hostile toward big business.[8] The antipathy of local businessmen to foreign investment has been expressed through pressure groups which have fused such a bond of administrative solidarity with certain ministries that both sides complain whenever other ministries interfere. This relationship has made it possible for disgruntled business groups to mobilize official backing for action in furtherance of primarily domestic business interests.[9]

Competition holds no allure for Frenchmen who equate it with the demise of the family-owned firm on the one hand and with industrial concentration on the other. The family-owned firm, of which there are an estimated 800,000,[10] is an institution which vast numbers of Frenchmen are dedicated to preserve. Efficient manufacture and distribution brought about by vigorous competition from large-scale enterprise would spell rapid attrition of small business. United States business is, of course, large-scale enterprise.

Attitudes Toward U.S. Enterprise

A vice president of the American Express Company, writing of obstacles to U.S. investment abroad,[11] told

[8] Henry W. Ehrmann, *Organized Business in France* (Princeton, N.J.: Princeton University Press, 1957), p. 137.

[9] Ehrmann, *ibid.*, pp. 233–234.

[10] *Ibid.*, p. 174.

[11] John W. Houser, "The Delicate Job of American Management

of a sampling of public attitudes taken in Europe in 1961:

A recent survey of public attitudes toward American business in France and Germany . . . showed that 58 per cent of the French opposed encouragement of the establishment of U.S. plants in France. Only 24 per cent favored encouragement. In Germany, 49 per cent were opposed, and only 19 per cent were favorably inclined.

He found that most unfavorable attitudes were tied to the fear of exploitation and to the feeling that American entrepreneurs are callous toward the local customs and ways of life. Businessmen obviously are not the only Frenchmen who prefer protection and security to competition and economic upheaval, progress notwithstanding.

Ehrmann, who has studied popular attitudes toward U.S. enterprise in France, has written of the aversion of Frenchmen toward "the Babel of modern materialism and senseless standardization."[12] They have viewed the American experience as without much significance for France, and attribute little of the U.S. standard of living to managerial policies or to production techniques. Frenchmen, he has found, ridicule management-labor relations for a "superficial cordiality" contrasting starkly with the layoff of thousands of workers from one day to the next.

Fear of antisocial or reckless industrial relations be-

Abroad," *Advanced Management — Office Executive,* January, 1962, pp. 20–21.

[12] Ehrmann, *op. cit.,* p. 325.

havior is therefore undoubtedly deep-seated among Frenchmen. The brusque decision of Remington to transfer its operations to another country struck many as typical of such behavior. The apparent disrespect for French ways aroused a resentment which will persist for years.

United States subsidiary firms have often bid up salaries and wages in labor-scarce areas in disregard of the government's interest in price stability.[13] This willingness and ability of U.S. subsidiaries to pay more and to price the product lower than others alienates the many smaller companies who compete with them. The financial resources available to them are seen to confer upon U.S. firms an advantage regarded as unfair.

Chauvinistic Feelings

French nationalistic pride has been buoyed in recent years by its expanding role in world affairs, its renewed stability, and its prosperity. Some part of French opinion is rooted in the ebullient belief of many ultranationalists that France should now liberate herself from U.S. influence, which at least one French author finds too pervasive.[14] Political parties at either end of the spectrum have declaimed the widely felt sense of dependency upon the United States. The hysterical newspaper attacks of January–February, 1963, certainly exhibit a marked anti-American feeling. It has even been suggested that the official statements of January, 1963, were

---

13 Gervais, *op. cit.*, p. 188.
14 Pierre Emmanuel, "Is France Being Americanized?" *The Atlantic Monthly, 201*:6, June 1958, pp. 35–38.

intended for no other reason than to arouse public support for President Charles de Gaulle's argument that Britain's entry into the EEC would pave the way for Anglo-American influence, which in the view of many is already too great.[15]

COUNTERVAILING INTERESTS IN U.S. INVESTMENT

To state that the French attitude is one of disaffection is to misrepresent greatly the genuine welcome which new U.S. direct investment has usually been accorded. Premier Pompidou himself acknowledged this in his news conference on February 5, 1963 when he said,

As for the American investments in Europe, particularly in Western Europe, we desired them, you know that, and on the whole they have had a certain number of salutary effects, particularly in awakening Europe's activity in some domains by providing it with the technological know-how and at the same time by giving it the capital it may have lacked in certain instances.[16]

A foreign investment office, the Bureau d'Accueil pour les Investissements Étrangers, was created in 1959 to encourage foreign investors in establishing operations in France. There are several underdeveloped regions in the country to which the government seeks to attract U.S. capital by means of special incentives. Lacking the venture capital needed to develop these areas,

[15] "Faut-il refuser les investissements américains en Europe?" *Enterprise*, No. 387, February 9, 1963, p. 13.
[16] At a luncheon given by the diplomatic press. "Speeches and Press Conferences No. 189," *Ambassade de France, Service de Presse et d'Information*, February 5, 1963.

the government has eagerly sought out American firms who desired to set up companies, subsidiaries, or to participate in existing French firms which the government deems too small or too numerous for economic operations.[17]

There are certain industries to which the French government is still anxious to attract U.S. capital. Generally speaking, these are industries that have received high priority in French economic planning, such as the machine-tool industry and tourism. United States companies investing in these fields would be encouraged, and possibly even subsidized, by the government. Moreover, the capital and technical contributions that sound U.S. investment can make are recognized as a major additional source of strength with which to meet vigorous competition within the Common Market.

[17] "French Offer Incentives to U.S. Investment in Distress Areas," *Foreign Commerce Weekly,* *62*:9, July 13, 1959.

CHAPTER FOUR

A Profile of United States Direct Investment in France

When French Finance Minister Valéry Giscard d'Estaing proposed that each member supply the EEC Commission with figures on third-country investment within its borders, he admitted that France had not yet compiled the called-for data. The only statistics which were available at that time had been published by the United States Department of Commerce, and they described only U.S. investment in France. Inasmuch as no officially authenticated statistics have been issued by the French government since d'Estaing made his proposal in March, 1963, the Department of Commerce figures stand as the single best official reference on the subject. Although the writings published in the interim period by Gervais and Bertin,[1] two learned French economists, rely heavily upon the Department of Commerce figures for their characterization of the part of U.S. investment in over-all foreign investment, they do add significantly to the lean body of statistical data

[1] Gervais, *op. cit.*, and Bertin, *op. cit.*

previously available. The material presented in this chapter is a composite of data taken from these sources.

Germane to a study of U.S. direct investment in France are such factors as the value and growth of the investment, its relative size in comparison with other foreign investment, and its contributions to the French economy. These and other factors are briefly examined in the following sections.

THE VALUE AND GROWTH OF U.S. DIRECT INVESTMENT

United States direct private investment has more than doubled since 1957 and is five times as great as it was in 1950. Table 1 shows both the value and growth of U.S. investment through 1962, when it reached $1,006 million. During the past five years, U.S. investors have poured in from $82 million to $149 million annually in fresh capital.[2]

The figures in Table 1 rank France after West Germany in terms of U.S. direct investment, a reversal of the rankings in 1950, twelve years earlier. France began to attract U.S. investment at the average rate for all six members of the EEC only after 1957, the inaugural year of the economic community, as may be seen from the per cent of increase over this period.

United States investment is small in comparison with that of neighboring European countries, whatever the criterion used. On the basis of U.S. investment per

---

[2] U.S. Department of Commerce, *Balance of Payments, Statistical Supplement* (Washington: Government Printing Office, 1962), pp. 208–209; and *Survey of Current Business*, Vol. 43, No. 8, August, 1963, pp. 18–19.

TABLE 1

VALUE OF UNITED STATES DIRECT INVESTMENTS IN EUROPE BY COUNTRY, 1929, 1936, 1943, 1950, 1957–1962 (Millions of Dollars)

Country	Y E A R										Per Cent of Increase	
	1929	1936	1943	1950	1957	1958	1959	1960	1961	1962	1950–57	1957–62
France	145	146	167	217	464	546	640	741	857	1006	215	217
Germany	217	228	513	204	581	666	796	1006	1177	1472	285	254
Italy	113	70	85	63	252	280	315	384	483	540	400	214
Netherlands	43	19	60	84	191	207	245	283	310	370	215	194
Belgium-Luxembourg	64	35	66	69	192	208	211	231	261	283	278	147
Common Market	582	498	891	637	1680	1908	2208	2644	3087	3671	263	218
United Kingdom	485	474	519	847	1974	2147	2477	3231	3542	3805	233	192
Europe Total	1353	1259	2051	1733	4151	4573	5323	6645	7713	8843	233	213

Source: *Balance of Payments, Statistical Supplement*, U.S. Department of Commerce, Washington, D. C.

capita, using 1961 figures, France ranks only before Italy, as the following table shows:

U.S. INVESTMENT PER CAPITA (1961)

United Kingdom	$66.50
Belgium-Luxembourg	27.50
Holland	26.30
Germany	21.50
France	18.20
Italy	9.40

That U.S. direct investment is growing at a rapidly accelerating rate is evident from Figure 1. If growth

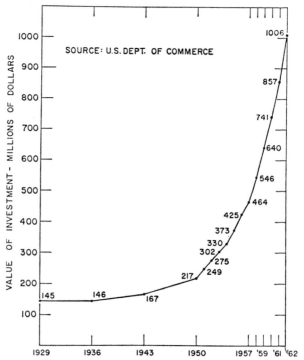

Figure 1. Value of United States Direct Investments in France, 1929–1962.

continues at the rate for the period 1957–1962, American investment will surpass $2.2 billion by 1967.

Table 2 shows the value of U.S. direct investments by major industries for the years 1950–1962, inclusive.

TABLE 2

VALUE OF UNITED STATES DIRECT INVESTMENTS IN FRANCE, BY MAJOR INDUSTRIES, 1950–1962 (Millions of Dollars)

Year	Manu- facturing	Petro- leum	Trade	Public Utilities	Mining & Smelt- ing	Other	Total
1962	582	257	122	10	9	26	1006
1961	469	248	95	10	9	26	857
1960	402	223	76	10	9	21	741
1959	342	201	61	10	8	19	640
1958	279	187	50	7	8	16	546
1957	243	155	42	3	8	13	464
1956	239	135	20	5	6	20	425
1955	213	113	18	5	6	18	373
1954	192	96	12	5	5	21	330
1953	175	90	11	5	4	18	302
1952	158	82	9	5	4	18	275
1951	137	82	7	5	3	15	249
1950	114	76	5	5	3	15	217

Source: *Balance of Payments, Statistical Supplement,* U.S. Department of Commerce, Washington, D. C.

Manufacturing has grown by five times during this period; the value of the petroleum industry investment has grown threefold. The greatest relative expansion has occurred in trade and distribution, which has risen from $5 million in 1950 to $122 million in 1962. The public utilities, and mining and smelting industries have grown but little because of the French legislative prohibitions excluding foreign participation in industries exploiting the natural resources of the country or in those touching activities vital to the public interest. Figure 2 illustrates the relative importance and growth of the major industries as parts of aggregate investment.

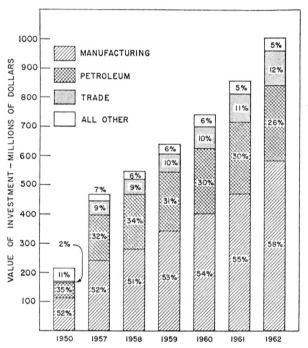

Figure 2. Value and Distribution as Per Cent of Total of United States Direct Investments in France, by Major Industries, Selected Years, 1950–1962.

The petroleum industry has declined in percentage of U.S. investment since 1957. Decrees issued in February, 1963, give the government-owned Union Générale des Pétroles a favored position for the period 1965–

1975, effectively curtailing future investment opportunities for the non-French petroleum companies. It seems likely, in view of this disability, that further growth in this industry sector of U.S. investment will be small.

The distribution of U.S. direct investment among major industries in Germany and Italy is very similar to that of France. No significant differences exist.

RELATIVE SIZE AND NUMBER OF U.S.-OWNED FIRMS

The number of French firms with U.S. direct equity participation has been variously estimated. Probably the most reliable estimate was obtained by adding 353, the number shown at the end of 1957 in the census[3] published by the U.S. Department of Commerce to 278, the number of new arrivals, in the years 1958–1962, according to the listing of the Chase Manhattan Bank prepared for internal use. Of the 631 firms so found to exist, probably only 400 are worthy of notice, the remainder having such a small scale of operations as to be inconsequential. In fact, the directory of the U.S. Embassy lists only 395 subsidiaries and branches of U.S. parent companies at the end of 1963.

Fewer than 200 of these companies are engaged in manufacturing according to a July, 1962, tabulation by the U.S. Chamber of Commerce. They are, however, largely the same companies which dominate *Fortune*'s directory of the largest industrial concerns in the United

[3] U.S. Department of Commerce, *U.S. Business Investment in Foreign Countries* (Washington: Government Printing Office, 1960), p. 99.

States. It is not surprising, therefore, that four of them should appear in a similar listing[4] of the twenty-five largest industrial companies in France, according to volume of sales.

A useful measure of the relative size of U.S. subsidiary companies is the number of employees on their payrolls. Table 3 lists the employment of the twenty-five largest U.S. subsidiaries in France. Only twenty

TABLE 3

THE TWENTY-FIVE LARGEST U.S. COMPANIES IN FRANCE, AS MEASURED BY EMPLOYMENT IN 1963

1.	Chrysler Corporation (Simca)	20,000
2.	International Telephone & Telegraph	9,250
3.	International Harvester Company	8,000
4.	International Business Machines Corporation	7,800
5.	Standard Oil Company (Esso Standard)	6,400
6.	Singer Manufacturing Company	6,200
7.	Eastman Kodak Company	5,500
8.	Mobil Oil Company	3,500
9.	General Motors Corporation	3,000
10.	Westinghouse Air Brake	3,000
11.	American Radiator (Ideal Standard)	2,500
12.	H. K. Porter (3 Companies)	2,350
13.	Otis Elevator Company	2,300
14.	Corn Products Company	1,800
15.	Timken Roller Bearing Company	1,660
16.	Norton Company (2 Companies)	1,650
17.	The Proctor & Gamble Company	1,400
18.	Minnesota Mining & Manufacturing Co.	1,400
19.	Crane Company	1,100
20.	The National Cash Register Company	1,050
21.	United Shoe Machinery Corporation (4 Companies)	990
22.	Charles Pfizer & Company	850
23.	Weyerhaeuser Company	750
24.	Union Carbide Corporation	700
25.	Fruehauf	600

[4] Appearing in "Report on Western Europe," a bimonthly communication to clients of the Chase Manhattan Bank, No. 24, June–July, 1963.

firms employ more than 1,000 workers. These twenty companies constitute the preponderance of U.S. investment in France.

Although he has not separately shown the growth of American companies, Bertin has vividly depicted the growing prominence of all foreign-owned enterprise in the French economy in these figures:[5]

FOREIGN COMPANIES

AMONG	In 1952	In 1956	In 1959	In 1961
50 Largest in France	8	8	7	8
100 Largest in France	15	16	18	18
500 Largest in France	—	35	41	56

Presumably, U.S. subsidiaries share in this growth in relative importance.

The number of new U.S. firms entering France annually has averaged between fifty and sixty over the past five years. Fifty-three new American firms established subsidiaries or branches in France in 1963, indicating that the attraction for that country continues to be strong.

EQUITY PARTICIPATION BY U.S. COMPANIES

United States direct investment has been made through acquisition of an existing affiliate, usually a licensee, by founding a new subsidiary, or by purchasing 25 per cent or more of the equity in a French company in which it had no prior financial interest. Before 1958, two-thirds of direct investments were made in existing af-

[5] Bertin, *op. cit.*, p. 246.

filiates. After 1958, four of every five investments were in new subsidiaries.[6]

Some data about U.S. ownership participation in French enterprise are presented in Table 4 together with

TABLE 4

PARTICIPATION IN INDUSTRY AND COMMERCE BY U.S. COMPANIES IN SELECTED COUNTRIES OF EUROPE IN 1962

	Per Cent of Companies with		
Country	*Majority Control*	*Minority Interest*	*Licensing Agreements Only*
Netherlands	61	33	6
Germany	49	37	14
Belgium-Luxembourg	48	32	20
Italy	39	46	15
France	39	45	16
Great Britain	32	44	24

Source: Chase Manhattan Bank

comparable information regarding other European enterprise. There is a significant difference from country to country in the percentage of U.S. parent companies with majority control of their subsidiaries. In France, U.S. investors hold majority shares in only 39 per cent of the cases. Similar data assembled by Bertin show that majority control is very frequent among the larger companies, in which the incidence of foreign majority ownership is two in every three.[7] There is evidence, too, that the preference for majority control of companies with

[6] "Les capitaux américains et l'industrie française," *Entreprise*, No. 362, August 11–18, 1962, p. 32.

[7] Bertin, *op. cit.*, p. 156.

U.S. equity participation is stronger in recent years than it may formerly have been.[8]

United States ownership of direct investment enterprises in France in 1957, as computed by the Department of Commerce, was $453 million as contrasted with French ownership of $491 million in the same companies. Of all outstanding equities in French companies in which U.S. investors have at least one-fourth ownership, 48 per cent is owned by U.S. investors.

CONCENTRATION IN PARTICULAR INDUSTRIES

Gervais, who has prepared the most extensive study of the concentration of foreign capital in French industries,[9] estimates the following percentages of output in specific industries to be produced by American-owned enterprise:

Carbon Black	95%
Synthetic Rubber	90%
Agricultural Implements	65%
Petroleum (Refining)	20%
Automobiles	15%

Reference to Table 5 shows that, of twelve branches of industry of which the foreign companies' share in production is 50 per cent or greater, U.S. companies may be said to have a dominant position in eight. As Gervais points out, however, it is easy to minimize or to exaggerate the share of U.S. investors in any industry,

[8] *Ibid.*, p. 158.
[9] Gervais, *op. cit.*, pp. 71–166.

TABLE 5

PERCENTAGE OF PRODUCTION OF FRENCH INDUSTRIES
UNDER FOREIGN CONTROL — APRIL, 1963

	Industry	Foreign Share of Production
1.	Photographic Supplies*	100%
2.	Carbon Black*	95
3.	Synthetic Rubber*	90
4.	Bearings	80
5.	Agricultural Implements*	70
6.	Telecommunications Apparatus	65
7.	Petroleum (Distribution)	65
8.	Elevators*	60
9.	Electric Lamps	50
10.	Office Machines*	50
11.	Tires*	50
12.	Valves*	50
13.	Automotive Parts	40
14.	Radio-Television	35
15.	Household Appliances	20
16.	Toys	20
17.	Machine Tools	20
18.	Petroleum (Refining)*	20
19.	Automobiles*	15

* Indicates Dominant U.S. Position in Foreign Share
Source: Gervais, La France Face aux Investissements Étrangers

depending upon the statistical base utilized.[10] For the percentages given in the previous paragraph, he has relied upon generally accepted unit measures of production as the base.

COMPARISON WITH OTHER FOREIGN INVESTMENT IN FRANCE

No statistical data has been published which discloses the value of total foreign investment in the major in-

[10] Ibid.

dustries, and for this reason it is impossible to determine the proportion which is of U.S. origin. Gervais has roughly estimated foreign investment in France not of U.S. origin, both direct and portfolio, to be in the order of $2.0 billion.[11] His estimate of U.S. investment on a comparable base is $1.7 billion. In direct investment, Great Britain ranks second, far behind the United States, with approximately $335 million in France; the Netherlands comes third, at $250 million. Portfolio investment, it is obvious, is proportionately much larger among other foreign investors.

Some figures have appeared for the years 1957–1960 that reveal the impact which foreign capital has had upon the formation of fixed capital in certain industries.[12] Foreign investors were responsible for 40 per cent of capital investment in the petroleum industries, 8 per cent in chemicals, 6 per cent in electrical equipment manufacture, and 5 per cent in the machine-tool industry.

GEOGRAPHIC DISPERSION OF FOREIGN-OWNED FIRMS

One foreign-owned firm in seven is located in Paris or its environs. A slightly higher number of these firms are owned by U.S. investors than are owned by other foreigners. Maps which have been prepared to show the dispersion of foreign-owned enterprise[13] reveal a preference among U.S. companies for the industrial centers of the North and East of the country.

11 *Ibid.*, p. 57.
12 Bertin, *op. cit.*, p. 219.
13 *Ibid.*, pp. 170–172.

Settlement of new foreign enterprise is now guided by the French Ministry of Industry and Commerce, which has been attempting to relocate industry outside the Paris area since 1945. Creation of new enterprise in the Paris area is subject to stringent authorization procedures; a number of incentives, for example tax relief and government grants, are offered to cooperating investors who agree to settle in the less developed areas. Prior to 1939, nearly half of all foreign-owned firms were located in the periphery of Paris.

MEASURABLE CONTRIBUTIONS TO THE FRENCH ECONOMY

Foreign direct investment in fixed capital assets, considered a good measure of its importance to the economy, was less than 3 per cent of total fixed capital formation in 1961, as Table 6 shows. Bertin concludes from these statistics that direct foreign investment is of little consequence,[14] although it must be observed that it is a factor of growing importance.

Direct employment is another measure of the contribution made by the foreign-controlled segment of the economy. According to Bertin, 60,000 new jobs were created by the direct employment of foreign companies establishing in France between 1958 and 1961.[15] Two-thirds of this total were in the Northeast quarter of the country. United States subsidiaries were estimated to employ in 1957 approximately 69,000 persons in

14 *Ibid.,* p. 214.
15 *Ibid.,* p. 226.

France[16] and 100,000 in 1962,[17] a number corresponding to less than 1 per cent of total employment. The number for all foreign enterprise, using their estimate, must be double that for the U.S. subsidiaries.

TABLE 6

FOREIGN DIRECT INVESTMENT IN FRANCE AS A PERCENTAGE OF FIXED CAPITAL FORMATION, 1954–1961

Year	Fixed Capital Formation (Per Cent)
1954	.06
1955	.11
1956	.28
1957	.38
1958	.72
1959	1.13
1960	2.43
1961	2.43

Source: Bertin, *L'Investissement des Firmes Étrangères en France.*

Wage and salary payments to workers in U.S.-owned business firms were $250 million in 1957. Purchases of materials and supplies worth $940 million and taxes totaling $314 million were also recorded for that year.[18] The sum of these disbursements exceeded $1.5 billion, an impressive amount.

[16] *U.S. Business Investment in Foreign Countries, op. cit.,* p. 122.

[17] Gervais, *op. cit.,* p. 62. The true figure is probably nearer 130,000.

[18] *U.S. Business Investment in Foreign Countries, op. cit.,* pp. 118–120.

CHAPTER FIVE

A Survey of External Management and Control of French Subsidiaries

Ministers of the French government have stated that France regards domination of certain sectors of industry by U.S. firms to be undesirable. A basic question to be considered, then, in judging the cogency of the official view, is the extent to which parent companies do control subsidiaries in France. How much of the decision-making power of management is shifted abroad when a U.S. company has acquired the majority interest was the focal object of the inquiry described in this chapter.

SURVEY METHOD AND OTHER PARTICULARS

The survey, conducted during January and February, 1964, consisted of a series of twenty-four separate interviews. Using a listing of U.S. companies with subsidiary operations in France, the interviewer selected fifty companies for the expressed purpose of obtaining data for a graduate research project. The writer's announced aim was to ascertain the views of U.S. companies concerning the change in attitude of the French government toward U.S. investments in that country. The letters, addressed to the executive responsible for the international operations of the company, asked for a discussion with that person in the parent organization directly responsible for the operation of the subsidiary. As an alternative, an interview with the official most closely associated with the management of the French company was requested.

Interviews were eventually held in twenty-four of the fifty companies solicited. In fifteen of the twenty-four cases, the respondent was the organizational superior of the manager charged with operating responsibility in France. The remaining nine respondents were either assistants of that organizational superior or other staff executives in the line of direct authority for French operations.

Each interview was prefaced by a brief explanation of the reasons why the subject was of wide concern. Not surprisingly, all but six of the respondents were roughly familiar with events which provoked French reaction. The precise objective of the interview was intentionally left vague until the conclusion of the talk in order to avoid a biased response. To encourage candor and to meet the wishes of one-fourth of the respondents, the writer assured each respondent that his identity would remain anonymous. The subject, it became apparent in several interviews, was sensitive and of intense interest.

Many of the companies interviewed were reappraising their investment plans in France.

Initially, an attempt was made to use a simple questionnaire. This effort was abandoned when it became evident that a structured discussion too often led the respondent away from disclosures which were highly relevant to the question of control. Instead, the interviewer led the discussion at appropriate junctures to a consideration of these questions:

1. Which company policies are formulated externally, i.e., by the parent company or an intermediate organization outside of France?
2. Which policy decisions are made autonomously by the subsidiary organization?
3. What are the techniques and instruments of control used by the parent company?
4. How does the parent company formulate policy decisions vitally affecting the French subsidiary's operations?

The conversation was led along these paths only after the respondent, at the writer's request, had described the company's operations in France. This procedure was found to be effective in provoking meaningful replies. More often than not, digressions turned up significant data and were, therefore, not discouraged; the elite group of executives interviewed would not have been quite as cooperative if guidance had been less subtle.

The writer took brief notes, with the permission of the respondent, during each interview. At a convenient time thereafter the notes were amplified into a more complete record of the discussions.

A DESCRIPTION OF THE COMPANIES SURVEYED

The companies surveyed were those with headquarter offices clustered in three major American cities in the East and Midwest. Companies in three large cities were chosen in order to maximize the number of interviews, with due regard for the time and funds allotted to the investigation. No attempt was made to select a cross section or scientifically constituted sample; the only criteria were those already mentioned, viz., subsidiary operations in France and location of parent offices in one of the three cities. Nor are the twenty-four companies an otherwise qualified group within the fifty to whom the requests for interview were mailed. They are the twenty-four companies whose executives were able and willing to submit to interviews at the times requested. The number would have been larger except for the constraint of time. Executives in international operations are especially prone to long absence from their offices; except for this the number of interviews would have been much larger.

Table 7 displays pertinent data characterizing the size of subsidiary company operations in France. The nature of the company's principal business, the annual dollar sales volume, the employment, and the percentage of U.S. ownership are shown for the subsidiary of each company interviewed. The total French employment of the respondent companies was approximately 60,000 people. Combined annual sales approached $1.5 billion, a not inconsiderable figure. The sample obviously included several of the largest subsidiaries of American companies doing business in France.

TABLE 7

NATURE OF BUSINESS, SALES VOLUME, EMPLOYMENT, AND OWNERSHIP OF COMPANIES INTERVIEWED

Company Number	Nature of Business	Annual Sales (Millions)	Number of Employees	Per Cent of Ownership	Year Interest Acquired	Title of Person Interviewed
1	Transportation Eqpt.	$ 5	350	100	1961	Board Chairman
2	Plumbing Supplies	60	2,500	100	1898	Exec. Ass't to Pres.
3	Aircraft Components	105	6,000	49	Prior to 1945	General Counsel
4	Paper Machinery	6	410	100	1958	Exec. Ass't to Pres.
5	Carbon Black	6	150	100	1955	Gen. Mgr. Overseas Div.
6	Motor Vehicles	589	20,000	64	1958	Vice Pres. — Int'l Ops.
7	Food Products	34	1,800	95	1927	Exec. Vice Pres.
8	Valves	5	1,100	76	1959	Controller
9	Appliances	74	3,000	100	1926	Regional Exec.
10	Toiletries	8	500	95	1914	Regional Exec.
11	Chemicals	10	475	51	1920	Pres. Overseas Div.
12	Household Products	7	125	100	1956	Regional Exec.
13	Business Machines	175	7,800	100	1914	Ass't to Pres.
14	Pharmaceuticals	3	225	100	1960	Director of Finance
15	Food Products	17	400	100	1961	Exec. Vice Pres.
16	Pigments	1	5	90	1928	Vice Pres. — Int'l Ops.
17	Elevators	20	2,300	99	1884	Vice Pres. — Int'l Ops.
18	Medicines	1	75	75	1961	Mgr. Overseas Div.
19	Beverages	1	150	100	1949	Ass't to Pres.
20	Pharmaceuticals	16	850	51	1954	Pres. — Int'l Ops.
21	Sewing Machines	57	6,200	100	1907	Ass't Vice Pres.
22	Petroleum Products	208	3,500	100	1913	Exec. Vice Pres.
23	Chemicals	12	700	60	1934	Regional Exec.
24	Machinery	8	1,000	100	1900	Ass't to Vice Pres.
All Companies		1,428	59,815			

The subsidiary companies may be broadly classified to fall within six categories. Eleven were durable-goods manufacturers and four were chemical companies. There were three pharmaceutical producers and three food processors. One company was engaged in both the refining and distribution of petroleum products. The remaining two companies made and marketed consumer soft goods.

The subsidiary companies varied greatly in size. Seven had more than 2,500 employees and sales in excess of $50 million annually; the smallest eight had fewer than 500 employees and annual sales under $10 million. The largest company had 20,000 employees; the smallest, 5.

United States equity participation ranged from 49 to 100 per cent of the shares outstanding. All French companies were operated as subsidiaries; every subsidiary was a *société anonyme,* or French corporation. In every instance the parent company held the controlling interest. The overwhelming majority of the respondent companies owned more than 75 per cent of the equity of the French subsidiary.

The parent companies had acquired their interests over a long span of years. The oldest dated back to 1884; the most recent, to 1961. Six had first invested prior to 1918; seven, in the period between world wars. Eleven had established a base of operations in France since 1945. Of the latter number, seven had entered France after the signing of the treaty creating the Common Market.

Of the parent companies interviewed, all but one are

to be found in *Fortune*'s directory of the 500 largest industrial firms in the United States.

FINDINGS OF THE SURVEY

For ease of comprehension, the composite response to the four broad questions posed is presented hereafter in separate sections. A final section treats in summary fashion the issue of parental authority–local autonomy. Interpretation of the consequences of the company practices revealed by the survey is reserved to the last chapter.

Policies Set by the Parent Company

Nearly all of the respondents answered that policy decisions involving outlays for capital items above a varying amount were taken by the parent company. Proposals to expand plants or to acquire new equipment ordinarily could be made only with the approval of a designated executive or committee of the U.S. company. Many executives noted that, while it was incumbent upon the subsidiary to take the initiative in submitting capital appropriation requests, the parent company retained the ultimate power of decision. One respondent had exercised this power to veto an expansion project submitted by its subsidiary a week before the interview. The parent finance committee had declined to authorize the expenditure upon grounds that the market potential for the product to be manufactured would not generate sufficient profitability for the investment.

Even after capital appropriation projects had received parent approvals, the companies in many cases continued to exercise control of policy. Respondents of Company 6 (automobiles) and Company 8 (valves) indicated that parental control was exercised in choosing sources of financing of new capital expenditures. The decision whether to borrow, and where to borrow, new funds was generally made by a financial manager of the parent company. The choice of equipment to be purchased was also often dictated by staff officials of the U.S. company. Respondents justified this control by arguing that cost and quality depended heavily upon the equipment used.

Dividend policy was similarly set by all of the parent companies. As in the case of capital appropriation requests, the subsidiary frequently prepared a recommendation to the appropriate financial manager of the parent, urging that a certain dividend rate be established. Many executives noted that, because of the French withholding tax upon dividend remittances to nonresident owners, the parent companies had advised subsidiaries to pass dividends if capital expansion programs were planned.

Control over financial matters was not restricted to capital expenditures and dividends. Company 5 (carbon black), with a handful of major customers competing with each other around the world, had had to centralize decisions over pricing in the parent company, the respondent said. Price disparities from one supplying location to another could have meant the loss of customers not only in France but elsewhere. Company 24 (machinery) also controlled prices from its U.S.

headquarters. Here again, its customers competed in several countries of the world; it could not afford to lease or to sell machines abroad at prices which gave foreign purchasers a competitive advantage over its larger U.S. customers. Company 9 (appliances) controlled all prices from the United States "as a matter of course," in the words of the respondent, who offered no justification for his company's policy.

Product policy was occasionally cited by the respondents as a matter exclusively for parent decision. Companies 14 and 20 (pharmaceuticals) decided which products of the lines developed by the parent company would be offered on the French market. This control extended to the claims made for the products offered, usually drugs, as well. Respondents pointed out that claims made for the products in the United States narrowed the claims which could otherwise have been made under applicable French law, upon ethical considerations. Likewise, other companies set rules for their French subsidiaries regulating the quality of products to be produced. Company 7 (food products) could not risk its reputation in the United States by distributing an inferior product abroad, because its name was too well known.

Most of the parent companies were multinational, and the executives interviewed often revealed that their companies were not simply domestically oriented. Nowhere was the global perspective — affecting parent company policy in France — more apparent than in their comments concerning manufacturing and supply. The executive of Company 13 (business machines) put it well in pointing to his company's decision to make computers in France, typewriters in Germany, and card tabulators in England. "Our foreign and domestic interests are woven into a net of integrated parts. By specializing in one product in France and another in Germany, we realize the economies of scale which the Common Market planners envisaged," he said. For Companies 11 (chemicals) and 12 (products for the home), France was just one of many markets. Each of these three parent companies had adopted policies restricting their French subsidiaries to the manufacture of specified product lines, leaving open the opportunity to acquire from sister companies products needed to supply French market demand.

Research and development was the subject of a number of externally imposed company policies. Several respondents said that company policy forbade research and development expenditures abroad because of company feeling that such expenditures were best made in a single location, preferably near parent offices.

Autonomous Local Decisions

In their replies to the query about which operational decisions were formulated autonomously, respondents most consistently cited sales, marketing, purchasing, personnel and labor relations, and production policies. There was no uniformity among respondents, however, that any one of these matters was to be left to the subsidiary for exclusive determination. All but a few agreed that day-to-day or short-term decisions should be left to the French company, but nearly every one called to mind notable exceptions evidencing parental interference in the decision-making process.

Company 9 (appliances), its regional executive said, left personnel matters to the local company. A few minutes later, he asserted that from time to time the parent company had found it necessary to order a reduction in personnel because of what he termed an "over-budget condition." A high executive of Company 13 (business machines) told an amusing story about a matter which had been taken to the president of the parent company himself for resolution. A financial analyst in parent headquarters, reviewing French purchasing statements, had noticed an accounting entry for wine. Inquiry showed the wine to have been served regularly in the company cafeterias, a not uncommon practice in France. It was brought to the attention of parent management, which decided after some deliberation, above the heads of competent local executives, to continue the practice.

Company 23 (chemicals), according to its respondent, required all labor agreements to be sent to the home offices, where they were reviewed prior to coming in force. The purpose, he said, was to bring practices abroad as nearly into conformity as might be feasible by issuing recommendations based upon experience in other locations. How heavy was the hand of parental influence did not become clear.

Another respondent, Company 10 (toiletries) said that the parent company, through its London regional office, influenced the working conditions of its 500 employees in France. He characterized the influence as "the type felt when you know your decision is subject to close review."

Policies adopted toward labor organizations were said to be locally decided in nearly every instance. Company 13 (business machines), whose domestic plants are not organized, has instructed its subsidiary to "keep unions out." The respondent hinted that the local executive would be ill-advised to suffer violation of the policy and that it doubtless influenced his every decision in labor matters.

One parent firm, Company 22 (petroleum products), had full control of any important operational decision made, its executive vice president said. He defended the practice by saying that the petroleum industry was a "sensitive" one in France and that overproduction or aggressive distribution methods could "upset the apple-cart." He commented that the government decrees of 1963 limit foreign oil companies to 40 per cent of the market. Instability in the foreign segment of the industry, he said, could result in further curbs.

Several respondents told the interviewer that compensation levels for key personnel in the upper strata of French management were set by the parent company. The suggestion was implicit that a few companies, at least, thought French salaries to be too low or too high.

There were other encroachments upon local autonomy in the matter of sales and production policies. Some parent companies dictated the number of salesmen to be employed. One had even issued, for a lengthy interval, production schedules for its subsidiary (Company 17, elevators).

Respondent for Company 2 (plumbing supplies) explained his company's interesting control philosophy. "We have adopted the concept that we are consultants to the subsidiaries. Upon request of the subsidiary, we will offer guidance using staff facilities in the U.S. company to coordinate, but not to control. The decision, whatever the problem, belongs to the local company." Four other companies gave a wide berth to subsidiary managers. These respondents said that they had learned after long experience that the local manager was nearly always in the most advantageous situation to "call the shots," with the exceptions already noted for capital improvements, expansion, and dividend policy.

Techniques of Control

The companies interviewed described three general means by which policy decisions or parental influence were transmitted to the subsidiary in France. Very important, in the opinion of most respondents, were the person-to-person contacts and correspondence between the parent officials and the management of the subsidiary. Most respondents visited France at least twice annually, and encouraged annual visits to the parent company by the ranking French executive, who was in all but five cases a national of France. Frequent visits by technical and staff representatives of the parent company also reinforced the line of control. Many respondents convened annual conferences of heads of all foreign subsidiaries to explain new corporate-wide aims, policies, and programs.

A second effective means was the widespread use of

policy manuals in which the parent company prescribed the procedures for handling a long list of situations, from which markets might be served by which subsidiary to the amount of severance pay to be given a discharged employee. Manuals ordinarily were prepared by staff departments of the parent company for the French controller or finance head and the general manager. In fourteen of the twenty-four companies, the manuals prescribed that capital expenditures above a certain amount required parental approval. Limits ranged from $250 (Company 17, elevators) to $25,000 (Company 11, chemicals). One executive, whose company manual set the limit at $15,000, called the limitation absurd, declaring that the company had allowed its French manager to build over $1 million in excessive inventories in the preceding year, but would not permit him to take out a lease of warehouse space to store it. Some companies left the local executive much leeway for the exercise of discretion.

The third method assuring adhesion to company policy was the use of the budget report. This report, often supplemented by others, such as working force reports or inventory reports, was required by more than half of the companies. The variance explanations, which respondents insisted accompany the comparisons of actual and planned performance, frequently stimulated the parent company to impose its wishes upon the French subsidiary. Too many indirect laborers or too much advertising expense, one respondent said, had brought an abrupt reaction from the parent company on more than one occasion.

How Parent Company Policy Was Decided

Respondents said that policy was usually adopted by executives of the parent company acting singly or in committee. Designated individuals usually were charged with the responsibility of preparing a recommendation to the decision-maker after consulting all affected departments and units of organization. Gentle probing by the questioner elicited the astonishing comment from one respondent (Company 3, aircraft components) that the French organization was not always consulted. The burden of explaining noncompliance belonged to the subsidiary, if the policy were unworkable or posed special difficulty. The advocate of French subsidiary interests in a significant number of cases was a member of the parent organization, whose point of view was frequently colored by his own status and unfamiliarity with all the considerations involved.

Typical Framework of Decision

Typically the parent company retained and exercised the power of ultimate decision over policies essentially financial in nature. New capital investment, dividends, sources of capital, and the assumption of long-term obligations, all were grist for the parent policy mill. Strategic planning in the allocation of corporate funds, including those of the subsidiary, the logistical flow of goods, pricing, and the production locale were matters ordinarily decided by the parent company.

French subsidiaries generally had operational responsibility for decisions concerning labor relations, sales, marketing, and production matters. From company to company, however, parent influence made itself felt on individual problems. The knowledge that local action was frequently subject to parent review certainly influenced local decisions in many cases.

The techniques and instruments of control often left little room for maneuver on policies on which the parent company had spoken. Budgetary control was used to influence action by most companies on matters not specifically covered by enunciated policy statements. The writer concluded from the interviews that, for at least one-fourth of the subsidiaries, local management enjoyed little autonomy on many issues of vital concern to France.

COLLATERAL FINDINGS

Much information collateral to that actually sought in the survey was given by respondents. Respondents, reflecting, perhaps, apprehension of some form of discriminatory action by the French, made spontaneous reference to pressures by groups in and out of French government that affected their operational policies. They also mentioned publicity, good and bad, that their respective companies had received in the French press. In the course of the conversations, many commented upon the effort a subsidiary had made to acquire and preserve French identity.

Pressures Observed by Respondents

The executive of Company 3 (aircraft components) said that the French government had taken pains to advise the subsidiary that any attempt to acquire a larger share of the equity would be unwelcome, even though with 49 per cent it had effective control. The company gave written assurance in 1958 that it would not. The subsidiary is a main supplier of critical aircraft parts to the government-controlled aircraft industry.

Another respondent, Company 8 (valves), acknowledged that French agencies seemed much more alert to the activities of U.S. investors than of other foreigners. He noted that their investment applications had met with much procrastination and delay, although approvals were eventually forthcoming. He would not describe these delays as harassment.

The regional executive of Company 9, an appliance manufacturer, complained that leftist unions were predisposed to invoke government review of any disputed grievance. He thought it might be a result of location in a communist-centered suburb of Paris, rather than evidence of a nationwide problem.

Company 15 (biscuits) had been refused an investment permit to acquire an insolvent food-processing firm, while the government, acting through the banking system, sought to interest French financial institutions in the failing firm. The government abandoned its search and granted the permit six months later.

The respondent for Company 20 (pharmaceuticals) declared that in 1953–1954 the French chemical and drug manufacturers' association importuned the Ministry of Finance to bar U.S. investment by American manufacturers in France, but to no avail.

Company 22 (petroleum), the executive said, was

often subjected to discrimination, as were all other producers in the industry. He smilingly added that the
company was willing to tolerate the discrimination because, once admitted to do business in France, it is so
very profitable.

Company 23 manufactured graphite electrodes, and
as the chief supplier to the French steel industry held a
near monopoly. The regional manager added that un-
named agencies of the French government would "step
in if the parent company tried to purchase the remaining
40 per cent of the shares in French hands."

Comments Regarding Publicity and Identity

Many respondents spoke proudly of long years of
operations in France without adverse publicity. Some
were so long established there that they could be, and
were, regarded as French. Company 2 (plumbing supplies), for example, had introduced central heating to
France in 1884 and was thought by most Frenchmen to
be a French company. The company, he said, did nothing to disillusion anyone on that score.

Company 7 (food products), also long established in
France, had the company name and all trade names put
in the French language in order to clothe itself with the
indicia of French identity. The vice president told the
writer that the company always conducted its operations
as a French company, taking care to abide by even those
social policies which were anathema to the parent company.

Company 10 (toiletries), a heavy advertiser, had felt
pressures from *L'Humanité*, the communist newspaper

in Paris. The newspaper had threatened at least once to "lambaste" the subsidiary if it continued to withhold advertising in its pages, promising to draw attention to its U.S. identity. The subsidiary did not submit.

One respondent, Company 14 (pharmaceuticals), followed as a standard practice the course of prior consultation with interested agencies of the government on developments of public interest. This habit had paid handsome dividends in favorable publicity in the trade press and in a willing response from the government when assistance was needed. He also thought the subsidiary should "act as the Romans, when in Rome."

The assistant vice president of Company 21 (sewing machines) emphasized the need to acquire French identity. His company had gone to the extreme of listing shares of the parent company on the Paris securities exchange in order to encourage the belief that the company is truly French. He emphasized also that local management had "standing orders to handle all personnel problems with a high degree of social responsibility."

Three subsidiaries had suffered adverse publicity when establishing in France. In each case the parent connection was publicized; but none of the three had observed any decline in business as a result.

THE IMA CASE STUDIES

The case studies of the International Management Association[1] reveal a similar pattern of parental control

[1] *Case Studies in Foreign Operations, IMA Special Report No. 1,* op. cit.

to that uncovered in the twenty-four–company survey. The executives quoted in the IMA cases were said to allow almost complete autonomy except in matters of financial policy. Financial policy, as defined by the IMA executives, was involved in any matter which the parent company thought deserving of control from the United States. While paying heed to the need for a maximum degree of local initiative and responsibility, most of the executives gave compelling reasons why new products, pension plans, compensation of personnel, etc., ought to be the primary business of the parent company. To this extent the findings of the earlier investigation are consistent with those presented here. They neither add to nor detract from the conclusions which may be drawn from this survey.

CHAPTER SIX

Vulnerability to New Regulation

The vulnerability of new direct U.S. investment to new regulation must be distinguished from that of existing investment to new regulation. Similarly, the capacity to adopt new regulation must be distinguished from the likelihood of new regulation. This chapter makes an assessment only of French capacity to regulate, saving the latter question for later evaluation. In proceeding to that assessment it should be remarked that legal impediments and other inhibiting forces do not of themselves guarantee the security of investment in a foreign country. The true bastion of security exists in the community of interest developed at the initiative of the investor within the host country.

CONTROL OF NEW INVESTMENT

Effective control of new direct foreign investment in France is accomplished by the imposition of restrictions or conditions on the entry of capital. In order to import his capital, a prospective foreign investor must secure the approval of the Ministry of Finance, Direction des Finances Extérieures. Authorization is required for the purchase of an interest in, or the creation in France of, a business concern; for the purchase of unlisted French securities or of foreign securities; and for any investment financed by contributions in kind, e.g., licensing of patents.[1]

For any direct investment of more than F.200,000 ($40,000) in an unlisted French company, approval of the Comité d'Investissement is required. This screening committee is made up of representatives of the Banque de France, Ministry of Finance, Commissariat Général au Plan, and other governmental institutions. All important investments are also reviewed at the technical or industry level and must bear the personal approval of the Minister of Finance.

France, in screening new investment, has exclusive competence to regulate all matters pertaining to the acquisition and transfer of property within its territory. Screening is recognized in international law as the right of sovereign states. It is not unlawful for it to require that no foreign-owned enterprises operate in certain industries, or that certain pursuits be open to its nationals only. It may even require as a condition of entry that resident citizens of France own a part of such enterprises.[2]

[1] United States Department of Commerce, "Establishing a Business in France," World Trade Information Service, *Economic Reports*, Part 1, No. 62–68 (Washington: U.S. Government Printing Office, 1962), p. 3.
[2] A. A. Fatouros, *Government Guarantees to Foreign Investors* (New York and London: Columbia University Press, 1962), p. 39.

France has historically exercised these rights to control investment in the extractive industries, in the public utilities industry, and in industries upon which the security of the nation depends. Heretofore, selection has rarely been arbitrary; applications have been rejected but for reasons easily deduced from the protection exercise of these rights affords. There is no appeal from a decision of the Ministry of Finance's denying approval. Screening is not regarded by the U.S. government as actionable discrimination, since no prior right exists. Even the Franco-American Treaty of Friendship, Commerce and Navigation,[3] which became effective on December 21, 1960, acknowledges the right of both nations to determine the extent to which aliens may acquire, manage, and control interests in sensitive industries.

REGULATION OF EXISTING INVESTMENT

Two important treaties concluded by France place France under certain disability to act unilaterally in the adoption of control over foreign investment, specifically U.S. investment. The first of these treaties is the Treaty of Rome, which gave birth to the European Economic Community on March 25, 1957. The second is the FCN treaty noted in the preceding section. Both figure heavily in any assessment of vulnerability to new control.

[3] "U.S. and France Sign Treaty Regarding Business Activities, Investments, and Personal Property Rights; with Text of Convention," *United States Department of State Bulletin, 41*:828–835, December 7, 1959.

The Treaty of Rome

Article 67 of the EEC agreement[4] provides that

1. Member States shall, in the course of the transitional period and to the extent necessary for the proper functioning of the Common Market, progressively abolish as between themselves restrictions on the movement of capital belonging to persons resident in Member States and also any discriminatory treatment based on the nationality or place of residence of the parties or on the place in which such capital is invested.

Article 70 prescribes that the EEC Commission, the administrative body under the treaty, shall propose to the Council of member states measures in regard to progressive coordination of exchange policies. Article 72 stipulates the obligation of member states to keep the Commission informed of any movements of capital to and from third countries, enabling the Commission to address to member states "any opinion which it deems appropriate on this subject." In these three articles reposes the restraint upon unilateral action hampering the French government.

Finance Minister Valéry Giscard d'Estaing, by appealing for collective action at the meeting of EEC foreign ministers in March, 1963, acted with reference to the treaty provisions. Without collective action France cannot enact measures the objectives of which are to discriminate against U.S. investment. Collective action is necessary to bar third-country capital from entry to the Common Market; France could act unilaterally

[4] Appearing in Part Two, Bases of the Community, Title III, The Movement of Persons, Services and Capital, Chapter 4, Capital, Treaty of Rome, March 25, 1957.

through stringent screening, but would probably only divert venture capital to another member country where it would eventually compete with French-based enterprise.

Under Article 86, abuse of a dominant position in the Common Market by member or third-country firms is the exclusive responsibility of the EEC Commission's Department of Competition. Even in the case of antitrust action, France is under some disability because of the requirement of collective action.

The FCN Treaty

Protection and encouragement of American private investment abroad have been, particularly since 1949, principal objectives of U.S. foreign economic policy. The United States has such treaties with three EEC members. The Franco-American treaty commits each country to accord within its territories to citizens and corporations of the other treatment no less favorable than that accorded its own citizens and corporations with respect to engaging in commercial, industrial, and financial activities. It formally endorses standards for the protection of property interests on legal and constitutional principles. It also recognizes the importance of furthering the international movement of investment capital.[5]

The provisions of the treaty are most strongly formulated to forbid the use of exchange restrictions solely in order to discriminate against investors in the transfer abroad of profits and capital. Restrictions are permitted

[5] U.S. Department of State, *op. cit.*, pp. 828–835.

when either state's monetary reserves reach a very low level.

The Treaty remains in force for an initial term of ten years and continuing thereafter unless notice of one year is given in advance of the date of intended termination by either party.

Legal Effect of the Treaties

The effectiveness of treaty promises should not be exaggerated. It is a comparatively simple matter for a country to adopt laws which ostensibly relate to both foreign and domestic investors, but which affect foreign investors more than domestic ones. The government of a capital-importing country can disadvantage foreign-owned enterprise in a myriad of ways. Import and export licenses, subsidies, and employment permits are only a few of the many levers of control which a country can manipulate. And a country's foreign exchange reserves may be made to appear as desired to justify its own purpose. It is often problematic, therefore, whether violation has occurred.[6]

There are nevertheless important legal effects. The first relates to the possibility of diplomatic intervention by the country of which the aggrieved investors are nationals. The second relates to the possibility of recourse to the courts of the host country. Treaties have the force of domestic law in both the United States and France, allowing foreign investors to invoke their provisions before a court or administrative agency. The third major

[6] Fatouros, *op. cit.*, pp. 219–220.

effect is to establish a number of conventional legal rules in areas in which preexisting customary rules were uncertain because of the sovereignty of states.[7]

France, unlike some states, has a record of fulfillment of treaty promises. It could not unilaterally abrogate its treaties with other states without violating international law.

French Inhibitions

Obviously, only serious aggravation would provoke France to ignore treaty promises. The reaction of foreign investors, certainly of U.S. investors, to a FCN treaty violation could lead to a significant decrease of private foreign investment in the offending nation, including that which it still desired. It could even result in economic pressures or sanctions by the United States. The government of France must take these considerations into account.

The reluctance, amounting even to opposition, of France's Common Market partners to restrict third-country investment is probably the single most important restraining force. West Germany, with its larger share of U.S. direct investment, has heretofore been unconcerned with the question of foreign control or domination. Italy and the Benelux countries are especially eager to attract more foreign capital, so great have been their needs for development. France cannot effectuate its aims on its own initiative until the other nations of the ECC are disposed to act in concert.

[7] *Ibid.*, p. 348.

WHAT THE FRENCH CAN DO

Screening, as outlined in the preceding section, is an effective means of control and will definitely be employed to greater advantage in the future in order to keep out unwanted new investment. While the desire to control existing foreign investment is constrained by the Treaties, there are a number of ways by which the government can bring pressure upon an offending company or group of companies.

Without violating its treaties, France can impose price controls upon a particular industry; price regulation is not unusual in France. It could adopt special regulations similar to those in force in the petroleum refining industry. Under its powers to govern in the general welfare, it could enact special legislation for the food and drug industries. By canceling orders from nationalized industries, by harassment through customs and tax authorities, and by requiring burdensome compliance with hundreds of obsolete laws, France could make routine operations difficult if the government thought that a company's activities conflicted with its objectives and priorities in the economic field.

By enacting legislation purportedly to regulate all companies, but having special effect upon a class of companies, the government could avoid, in part at least, the treaty prohibitions. One often-proposed measure would grant plural voting rights to French residents or to stockholders who have held shares for more than a stipulated period, say for five years. Such a law would clearly deprive Chrysler, for example, of its recently acquired 63.8 per cent majority control and was probably proposed in reaction to it. Re-enactment of the law repealed on April 26, 1930 that allowed foreigners to hold only nonvoting shares is not regarded as likely.

CHAPTER SEVEN

Conclusions and Recommendations

From the material set forth in earlier chapters, several conclusions emerge to broaden understanding of the subject matter under study. The conclusions generally support the views of French officials, in the writer's opinion. It remains only to present these conclusions, in summary form, and to make certain recommendations based upon them for the benefit of the investing companies, the French government, and those interested in further exploration of the subject.

FINDINGS OF THE STUDY

The anxiety of the French government first became evident in the autumn of 1962, when the subsidiaries of two U.S. companies announced decisions to discharge a large number of workers without invoking the assistance of the government to find some other solution. The later acquisition of Simca majority control by Chrysler and the activities of other U.S. companies in seeking acquisitions combined with growing political friction over the entry of Great Britain into the Common Market to produce an extreme reaction well out of proportion to the events themselves.

This reaction was symptomatic of a change in French attitudes that has reflected not only official concern for the integrity of French planning, but also popular fear of competition from larger American companies. To some degree the facts warrant an inference of irrational and unabashed nationalism, a feeling which has mounted steadily with the economic growth and stability of France stemming from the de Gaulle reforms of 1957–1962. The claim that external control is often exercised in a manner inimical to legitimate national interests is certainly ill-supported by the isolated case of Remington Rand. The resultant effect of the furore has been to obscure the real and continuing interest of the French government in attracting U.S. capital to certain industries and to underdeveloped areas of France.

United States direct investment in France seems relatively small, tending to undermine the French allegation that U.S. capital has a dominant position in the economy. France, it has been seen, ranks next to last among Common Market countries in U.S. direct investment per capita. It accounts for less than 28 per cent of all U.S. investments in the Common Market and only 11 per cent of aggregate U.S. investments in Europe. United States companies produce less than 2 per cent of the French gross national product. The charge that there is a heavy concentration of United States capital in specific industries is amply borne out by the facts, on the other hand.

Whether these industries are critical to the French economy is a matter of opinion.

The gravamen of the French complaint — that U.S. companies exercise undue control of their subsidiaries — received decided confirmation from the survey. In a significant number of companies, on policy matters touching upon activities vital to the French economy, there was little delegation of authority to subsidiary management. Respondents agreed unanimously that the paramount function of control is to relate the financial investment in the French plant to the ultimate size and potential of French operations, but most of them admitted that control served other purposes, e.g., to coordinate production among several European plants. The centralization of the decision-making process in the United States appears to be particularly objectionable in view of the offhand manner in which decisions of great consequence abroad are frequently made. This casual approach to decisions involving international business, more often than not a small part of a company's total business, has been noted elsewhere.[1]

The survey disclosed virtually no evidence of discrimination or harassment by French authorities, once a company had been admitted into France. There was a preponderance of opinion that a foreign company should do everything possible to identify its venture with the purposes of the host country.

In view of the treaties and of the necessity for collec-

[1] Richard D. Robinson, *International Business Policy* (New York: Holt, Rinehart and Winston, 1964), pp. 217–218.

tive action by Common Market members it seems quite
unlikely that France will alter its investment control
procedures. Judged by its actions since February, 1963,
France will henceforth rigorously apply its criteria for
investment, restricting unwanted U.S. companies from
entry, and channeling others into welcome areas of activity. The French may be relied upon, under de Gaulle,
to continue the campaign against U.S. direct investment
within the Common Market. The odds are slight that
other EEC countries will act with France to foreclose
U.S. investment; as long as American companies can
establish freely in other countries of the Common Market and penetrate France through exports, there is little
that it can, or will, do alone. Its concern, moreover,
seems less with the volume of U.S. capital investment
than with its concentration and with the practices of certain U.S. companies. Careful screening should prevent
further concentration in given industries. Regulatory
measures beyond the pale of contemplation may be
devised in the event of a recurrence of activities like
those of Remington, which are deemed to be at odds
with national policy.

There is nothing either in the press accounts of the
activities of U.S. investors or in the explanations of
French officials to support the allegation that whole sectors of the economy have been removed from the reaches
of the national planning authority, to the detriment of
France's economic objectives. Aside from the issue of
whether whole sectors of the economy are under U.S.
control, this charge presupposes an intention by many
companies acting in concert to thwart or to ignore the

national purpose. It is, therefore, an unwarranted pre-supposition.

RECOMMENDATIONS

The conclusions and inferences which have been drawn from the data evoke certain recommendations, suggesting appropriate action for U.S. companies with investments in France and provoking a call for clarification of the government's position.

For U.S. Investors

United States companies with direct investments in France are well advised to conduct their business in harmony with the economic interests and social values of the host country. In the long run, the success of any American enterprise abroad depends upon its relations with the people of the country. Its permanence and freedom of operation will be related to the importance of its contributions to the social development of France; long-run survival demands that it refrain from actions which conflict with those prescribed for similar national firms. In short, American enterprise must forgo the latitude which U.S. economic policies would allow in order to acquire the moral position in France that makes drastic interference with its interests unlikely.

Legal guarantees cannot by themselves create the community of continuing interests between U.S. investors and France which is the real basis of the investor's security. Specifically, this means paying no more than the prevailing wage rate in a tight labor market or discharging workers only after full compliance with all administrative requirements and official review. It may also mean genuine cooperation in the industry commit- tees that decide branch-by-branch targets and implemen- tation of the economic plans, even where cooperation implies abandonment of individual company goals. Nothing more is requested than the qualification that subsidiary business operations broadly coincide with the development aspirations of France, so that conflicts of interest between the company and the government are minimized. A foreign company is operated wisely which conforms not only to the letter of the law in the host country but also to the spirit of the law and the ideals of the people upon whom it depends. Ralph J. Cordiner, Chairman of General Electric Company, expressed it as follows:[2]

The key to survival is this: to make the company so visibly useful, not only to the few who may be in power, but to the fundamental needs of the people in that country that the busi- ness rests on a basis of popular support and usefulness which all politicians feel obliged to respect.

Where its plans and interests diverge from those of the economic plan, a subsidiary company should scrupu- lously explain its nonconformity to the government agencies affected and, if necessary, to the general public. When it must act contrary to the advice of government, it should do so only after having exhausted all attempts

[2] Ralph J. Cordiner, "Managerial Strategy for International Business," an address before the World Trade Dinner, National Foreign Trade Council, *Vital Speeches*, 27:248–52, February 1, 1961.

at reconciliation of its views with those of the planners and administrators, with careful consideration of proffered governmental assistance. It is conceivable that, in time to come, when the four-year plans are no longer self-fulfilling, a company will be asked to increase its capital outlays in spite of doubtful profits. A high order of business diplomacy will be necessary in such a situation.

It behooves U.S. investors to re-examine the system by which control is exercised and to inquire of themselves why controls have been adopted. It is not enough to state that controls are needed to insure development and implementation of policies compatible with fundamental objectives, or to provide a means by which the parent company can judge the performance of the subsidiary and its management. Parent companies must, in their own enlightened self-interest, deliberately circumscribe those operational problem areas in France which require an expertise or familiarity lacking in headquarters personnel; they must delegate full authority in them to subsidiary management. This is not to say that they should not require that parent companies be kept fully informed on matters vital to its investment and its reputation.

Even more important, every parent company should delineate those operational decisions which it must take, carefully considering the complexity of interorganizational relationships, the nature of its business, and the desirability of decentralized operations. The essential decision areas for most companies will include the selection of executive personnel, capital appropriations, dividends, research and development expenditures, and product choices. The list of decision areas will necessarily differ from company to company; there are no real absolutes. There is, however, a presumption that a larger degree of decentralization in the decision-making process is to be preferred to a smaller degree. While certain central organization functions are essential to the logical development and proper control of a company's activities, sound business administration at the subsidiary level requires a generous grant of authority and independence.

Decentralized authority clearly runs fewer risks of offending the host country. Nevertheless, it cannot be said that the authority conferred by the parent company should depend upon the chauvinistic outlook of any given people at any given time. The principles set forth in the preceding paragraphs are as applicable and appropriate for France as they are for Great Britain or Germany. The wisest policy is one that is universally valid.

The insistence of many of the respondents in the survey that centralized control is necessary to coordinate company strategy in the execution of global activities suggests that a professionalization is also necessary in international management, not only abroad but in the United States as well. Decisions which are laden with unfortunate consequences in a foreign country can be avoided by those with the insight which can be gained only through long experience abroad. International business affairs seems to be too often influenced by men who are not knowledgeable of the country in which an apparently minor decision can have tremendous, unforeseen impact.

United States companies desiring to make future direct investments in France should consider the joint venture as an appropriate form of business participation. Joint ventures with local investors evoke greater friendliness on the part of the government and create an incentive in the government to avoid actions damaging to the venture, since local investors' interests will also be impaired. By associating with local investors, U.S. companies can enhance their position to influence favorably government policies and treatment. The burden of management is certainly more onerous, but vulnerability is significantly decreased.

Most U.S. investors will seek majority participation in a joint venture in order to acquire control. In doing so, investors are well advised to recognize that, even in France, where minority shareholders have the right to little more than the annual balance sheet, a brief auditor's report, and the formal statements of the board, a disgruntled local minority can be a dangerous thing. There is a potential conflict of interest in such matters as the rates of reinvestment of earnings and of dividend distribution which requires an engineering of consent. The joint venture is both a financial partnership and an experiment in human cooperation. When successful, it can provide the most secure and rewarding base for business operations in a foreign country. When unsuccessful, it can become an exercise in frustration, making the tasks of administration infinitely more difficult. Those companies who choose the joint venture should take care to explain and justify company policies to the minority, counting the wear and tear on management as a real cost of operation but one well worth the expenditure.

One authority on international investment[3] contends that whatever the attitude toward shared ownership, the long cherished doctrine of full ownership and control of overseas investments must eventually give way to the joint venture. He argues that U.S. firms operating abroad should view their role more "in terms of entrepreneurs seeking to mobilize domestic resources while using foreign capital and skills as catalysts." Granted that this view, ignoring as it does the profit motive, is altogether too altruistic for U.S. business, no better answer lies in the statement that foreigners are always free to purchase shares in the U.S. parent company. Local investors are poorly situated, generally, to acquire such interests, not to mention the difficulties they would encounter in staying informed of company activities. Irrespective of their preference, many U.S. companies must adopt innovations in ownership policy and in organization structure if they are to achieve some balance between profits and security. Adherence to the principle that all foreign enterprise must be wholly owned by the

[3] Raymond F. Mikesell (ed.), *U.S. Private and Government Investment Abroad* (Eugene, Oregon: University of Oregon Books, 1962), p. 584.

parent company ignores or avoids the national pride and sensitivity of the people in most host countries.

For the French Government

United States investors would welcome a clear statement of policy by the French government of the industries in which U.S. direct investment is desired. Investment presupposes a basic political evaluation which would benefit from such a definition. It would eliminate wasteful searching for opportunities by informing foreign investors that the field of interest is either open or closed. In addition to dispelling the doubts of potential new investors, a positive expression would tend to reestablish the equilibrium lost by so many French observers during the early months of 1963.

A leading banker in Canada, another country recently disturbed by U.S. control of local industry, could well have been speaking for U.S. investors and to the French government, instead of his own, when he urged:[4]

This is basically a political problem: a problem of maintaining national sovereignty, of being master in our own house. . . . If we are concerned about the behavior of foreign-owned subsidiaries — now or in the future — let us secure through moral suasion or appropriate legislation the kind of behavior we want. The foreign parents as well as their Canadian children would probably welcome a clarification of their position and a removal of the uncertainty which now arises from much grumbling but no clear-cut definition of where they stand and where we stand . . . the government, in ensuring a high degree

4 *Ibid.*, p. 492.

of Canadian economic independence, need not resort to any tinkering with exchange rates, trade balances or capital flows . . . .

THE UNANSWERED QUESTIONS

At least two important questions have been suggested to the writer in the course of his investigation. They have not been answered by the study, nor even precisely formulated. Because they are important and because more knowledge of the whole subject of international business management is sorely needed, the writer proposes these two questions for future research. Answers, if obtained, would serve a broader purpose than those given in the introduction to this study.

The actions of a single firm in reassigning its French production to another foreign plant showed dramatically one way in which the actions of a multinational company can come into conflict with a legitimate foreign, national interest. Other activities, like the constant transfer of liquid funds from one country to another, are also potentially troublesome. How the desire of multinational companies to maximize their resources can be realized without jeopardizing their welcome abroad or colliding with foreign governments is one question begging for an answer. Useful research on this subject would include a compendium of the methods by which multinational companies do make fullest use of their assets abroad.

A second question, how to reshape the organization structure and redraw lines of responsibility to give effect to the internationalization of U.S. companies, also conspicuously merits further research. Conventional organization structures in American companies that derive a rapidly expanding share of their income from operations abroad are obsolete. International operations cannot continue to be, as it is in many companies, an oddly related appendage off the lower corner of the organization chart. It must be integrated in the framework of organization so that worldwide responsibilities are shared by all line and staff departments. Effective organizational relationships could prevent the kind of management action which precipitated the crisis over U.S. investment in France. The importance of finding a solution to the problem demands that more research be devoted to it.

Classified Bibliography

PUBLIC DOCUMENTS

France. Journal Officiel. Avis et Rapports du Conseil, Économique et Social. Compeyrat, J. F. "Étude sur l'Opportunité et les Modalités de l'Investissement de Capitaux Étrangers en France Métropolitaine," January 3, 1959, pp. 1012–1036.

U.S. Department of Commerce. *Balance of Payments, Statistical Supplement, Revised Edition.* A Supplement to the Survey of Current Business. Washington: Government Printing Office, 1962. 260 pp.

U.S. Department of Commerce. *Doing Business with France.* Washington: Government Printing Office, 1958, viii, 122 pp.

U.S. Department of Commerce. "Establishing a Business in France," World Trade Information Service, *Economic Reports*, Part I, No. 62–68, Washington: Government Printing Office, 1962.

U.S. Department of Commerce. "Expansion in U.S. Investments Abroad," *Survey of Current Business*, August, 1962, pp. 18–24. 252 pp.

U.S. Department of Commerce. "Financing U.S. Direct Foreign Investment," *Survey of Current Business*, September, 1962, pp. 17–23.

U.S. Department of Commerce. "Foreign Operations of U.S. Industry," *Survey of Current Business*, October, 1963, pp. 13–20.

U.S. Department of Commerce. *U.S. Business Investment in Foreign Countries.* A Supplement to the Survey of Current Business. Washington: Government Printing Office, 1960. 147 pp.

U.S. Department of Commerce. "U.S. International Investments," *Survey of Current Business*, August, 1963, pp. 16–22.

U.S. Department of State. "U.S. and France Sign Treaty Regarding Business Activities, Investments, and Personal Property Rights; with Text of Convention," *U.S. Department of State Bulletin*, 41:828–835, December 7, 1959.

U.S. Department of State. "United States and France Exchange Ratifications of Convention of Establishment," *U.S. Department of State Bulletin*, 43:902, December 12, 1960.

U.S. Embassy to France. "Economic Summary, Fourth Quarter, 1962, First, Second, Third and Fourth Quarters, 1963," unclassified reports to the U.S. Department of State.

BOOKS

Aitken, Thomas. *A Foreign Policy for American Business*. New York: Harper & Row, 1962. 159 pp.

Baum, Warren C. *The French Economy and the State*. Princeton: Princeton University Press, 1958. 391 pp.

Bertin, Gilles-Y. *L'Investissement des Firmes Étrangères en France*. Paris: Presses Universitaires de France, 1963. 324 pp.

Comité Franc-Dollar. *Business Operations in France, A Guide for American Investors*. Washington: Comité Franc-Dollar, 1961. vi, 55 pp.

Ehrmann, Henry W. *Organized Business in France*. Princeton, N.J.: Princeton University Press, 1957. 514 pp.

Fatouros, A. A. *Government Guarantees to Foreign Investors*. New York and London: Columbia University Press, 1962. 411 pp.

France, Boyd. *The Case Study of IBM in France. Studies in United States Business Performance Abroad*. Washington: National Planning Association, 1961. 85 pp.

France's Fifth Republic and the Business World. Geneva: Business International, 1963. 72 pp.

Friedman, Wolfgang G., and George Kalmanoff (eds.). *Joint International Business Ventures*. New York and London: Columbia University Press, 1961. 558 pp.

Friedman, Wolfgang G., and Richard C. Pugh (eds.). *Legal Aspects of Foreign Investment*. Boston: Little, Brown and Company, 1959. 812 pp.

Gervais, Jacques. *La France Face aux Investissements Étrangers*. Paris: Éditions de l'Enterprise Moderne, 1963. 235 pp.

Hackett, John, and Anne-Marie Hackett. *Economic Planning in France*. London: G. Allen & Unwin, 1963. 418 pp.

Hauser, Rita E., and Gustave M. Hauser. *A Guide to Doing Business in the European Common Market: France and Belgium*. New York: Oceana, 1960. 271 pp.

Hoffmann, Stanley, and others. *In Search of France*. Cambridge: Harvard University Press, 1963. 443 pp.

Madeheim, Huxley, Edward M. Mazze, and Charles S. Stein (eds.). *International Business — Articles and Essays*. New York: Holt, Rinehart and Winston, 1963. 229 pp.

Mikesell, Raymond F. (ed.). *U.S. Private and Government Investment Abroad*. Eugene, Oregon: University of Oregon Books, 1962. 599 pp.

Robinson, Richard D. *International Business Policy*. New York: Holt, Rinehart and Winston, 1964. 252 pp.

Sheahan, John. *Promotion and Control of Industry in Postwar France*. Cambridge, Mass.: Harvard University Press, 1963. 301 pp.

PERIODICALS

"All gall: French Subsidiaries of General Motors and Remington Rand Lay Off Workers," *Time*, *80*:88, September 21, 1962.

"Business Abroad — Is Europe Still a Good Business Bet?" *Business Week*, February 9, 1963, 88–91.

"Canada Asks: Who Controls?" *Business Week*, February 25, 1961, p. 56.

104   CLASSIFIED BIBLIOGRAPHY

"Capital Gain: French Plan to Curb American Investment in Europe," *Newsweek*, *61*:68–69, April 8, 1963.

"Chrysler Exploits Simca Deal," *Business Week*, October 25, 1958, p. 102.

"Chrysler Move Rouses France," *Business Week*, January 26, 1963, p. 100.

Cordiner, Ralph J. "Managerial Strategy for International Business." An address before the World Trade Dinner, National Foreign Trade Council. *Vital Speeches*, *27*:248–252, February 1, 1961.

"De Gaulle and French Industry — A Glint in the Patronat's Eye," *Economist*, *206*:340, January 26, 1963.

"De Gaulle Slows Anti-Yanqui-Investor Campaign," *Business International*, March 29, 1963, p. 7.

Emmanuel, Pierre. "Is France Being Americanized?" *The Atlantic Monthly*, *201*:35–38, June, 1958.

"Faut-il refuser les investissements américains en Europe?" *Entreprise*, No. 387, February 9, 1963, p. 13.

"France Adds Muscle to State Oil Companies by Curbing Its International Rivals," *Business Week*, July 4, 1964, p. 78.

"France — The Power and the Commerce," *Economist*, *206*: 495–496, February 9, 1963.

"Freedom to Fire in France: Denouncement of General Motors and Remington Rand for Announced Layoffs," *Business Week*, September 22, 1962, p. 96.

"French Motors — Manufacturers on Their Guard," *Economist*, *207*:273, April 20, 1963.

"French Offer Incentives to U.S. Investment in Distress Areas," *Foreign Commerce Weekly*, *62*:9–11, July 13, 1959.

Grenier, Richard. "U.S. Investments in France," *The Reporter*, *28*:23–25, June 6, 1963.

Houser, John W. "The Delicate Job of American Management Abroad," *Advanced Management — Office Executive*, January, 1962, pp. 20–21.

"Les capitaux américains et l'industrie française," *Entreprise,*
No. 362, August 11–18, 1962, pp. 3–42.

"Multi National Companies: How U.S. Business Goes World-
Wide," *Business Week,* April 20, 1963, pp. 62–86.

Randall, Clarence B. "How to Get Along Overseas," *The Atlantic Monthly, 203*:51–54, March, 1959.

"The Resurgence of Nationalism in Gaul: De Gaulle Glowers
at U.S. Investors," *Business International,* February 1,
1963, pp. 1–2.

"Thwarted U.S. Firm Takes Ingenious Road to France," *Business International,* May 17, 1963, p. 2.

"U.S. Broadens Trade with France; Investment Outlook
Bright," *International Commerce, 68*:32–34, June 25,
1962.

Vernon, Raymond. "Saints and Sinners in Foreign Investment," *Harvard Business Review, 41*:146–161, May,
1963.

"Where Welcome Sign Is Coming Down for U.S. Dollar," *U.S.
News & World Report, 55*:66–68, July 8, 1963.

"Yankee Dollars in Europe," *Newsweek, 61*:78, February 11,
1963.

REPORTS

International Management Association. *Case Studies in Foreign Operations. IMA Special Report No. 1.* New
York, published by American Management Association, 1957. 237 pp.

International Management Association. *Applying Financial
Controls in Foreign Operations. IMA Special Report
No. 2.* New York, published by American Manage-
ment Association, 1957. 177 pp.

International Management Association. *Increasing Profits from
Foreign Operations. IMA Special Report No. 3.* New
York, published by American Management Associ-
ation, 1957. 240 pp.

NEWSPAPERS

Le Monde, September, 1962–March, 1963.
Le Figaro, January–March, 1962.
The Wall Street Journal, October, 1963–September, 1964.

INDEX

Equity participation, by acquisition, 49, 50
  proportion of, 51
  in selected countries, 50
European Economic Community, 13, 17–18, 21, 23, 42, 79, 81, 83, 88, 90
Exchange controls, 35, 80, 81

Family-owned firm, 36
Fears, of antisocial behavior, 38
  of big business, 36
  of competition, 20, 23, 35, 36, 38
  of concentration, 27
  of exploitation, 37
  of noncooperation, 30, 31
  official, 3, 4, 35
  of overcapacity, 32
Financial institutions, 31
Fixed-capital formation, 53, 54, 55
Food-processing industry, 19, 20, 33, 84
Ford Motor Company, 32
Foreign exchange reserves, 23, 35, 82
Foreign-owned enterprise in France, 49, 50, 53
  geographic dispersion of, 53–54
Four-year plans, 31, 93
French government, attitude of, toward concentration of foreign investment in key industries, 27
  toward U.S. investment, 3, 97
French identity of foreign companies, 72, 74–75, 89
French press, 7, 15, 20, 22, 38, 72, 90

General Electric Company, 25, 26
General Motors France, 13, 14, 16, 19, 24
German attitude, 21, 37
Gervais, Jacques, 8, 41, 51, 53

IBM of France, 25
IMA case studies, 8, 75–76
Incentives to invest, 39, 54

Investment, criteria for approval, 23, 24, 26, 28, 32, 34, 78, 90, 97
  in fixed assets, 54
  security of, 77, 81, 91
Investment application, 20, 24, 25, 73, 77–79
Investment policy, French, 22–24, 26, 28

Joint venture, 26, 95, 96

Labor shortage, 16, 38
Layoff of work force, 14, 15, 17
Libby, McNeill & Libby, 19, 20, 24
Local decisions, 66–69, 71–72, 93
Local management, 7

Machines Bull, 25, 26, 33
Machine-tool industry, 40, 53
Majority control of subsidiaries, 50, 87
Management-labor relations, 37
Massé, Pierre, 31, 32
Maurice-Bokanowski, Michel, 15, 17, 28
Ministry of Agriculture, 19
Ministry of Finance, 18, 19, 21, 23–25, 73, 78–79
Ministry of Industry and Commerce, 15, 24, 54
Ministry of Labor, 15
Minority shareholders, 95

Nationalism, 38, 88

Official guidelines, 32, 78
Official statements, 15, 18, 25, 27, 31, 38, 39
Organizational relationships, 98, 99
Ownership, French, as prerequisite for investment, 24, 78
Ownership policy, 95, 96

Parental control of subsidiaries. See Subsidiaries
Petroleum industry, 33, 34, 45, 46, 47, 52, 53, 68, 74, 84

Date Due

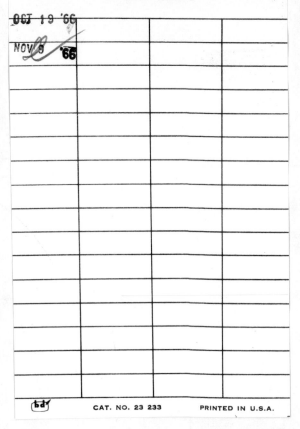